THE BIG
FOUR

Also by S. Joseph Kidder:

Majesty

To order, call **1-800-765-6955**.

Visit us at
www.reviewandherald.com
for information on other Review and Herald® products.

THE BIG FOUR

Secrets to a Thriving Church Family

S. JOSEPH KIDDER

REVIEW AND HERALD® PUBLISHING ASSOCIATION

Since 1861 | www.reviewandherald.com

Published by Review and Herald® Publishing Association, Hagerstown, MD 21741-1119

Review and Herald® titles may be purchased in bulk for educational, business, fund-raising, or sales promotional use. For information, e-mail SpecialMarkets@reviewandherald.com.

The Review and Herald® Publishing Association publishes biblically based materials for spiritual, physical, and mental growth and Christian discipleship.

The author assumes full responsibility for the accuracy of all facts and quotations as cited in this book.

Unless otherwise indicated, Bible texts are from the *Holy Bible, New International Version.* Copyright © 1973, 1978, 1984, 2011 by Biblica, Inc. Used by permission. All rights reserved worldwide.

Texts credited to KJV are from the King James Version.
Scripture quotations marked NASB are from the *New American Standard Bible,* copyright © 1960, 1962, 1963, 1968, 1971, 1972, 1973, 1975, 1977, 1995 by The Lockman Foundation. Used by permission.
Texts credited to NKJV are from the New King James Version. Copyright © 1979, 1980, 1982 by Thomas Nelson, Inc. Used by permission. All rights reserved.
Bible texts credited to RSV are from the Revised Standard Version of the Bible, copyright © 1946, 1952, 1971, by the Division of Christian Education of the National Council of the Churches of Christ in the U.S.A. Used by permission.

This book was
Edited by Gerald Wheeler
Copyedited by James Cavil
Cover art and design by Lars Justinen/jcg.com
Typeset: Bembo 11/13

PRINTED IN U.S.A.

15   14   13   12   5   4   3

Library of Congress Cataloging-in-Publication Data
Kidder, S. Joseph, 1953-   .
   The big four : secrets to a thriving church family / S. Joseph Kidder.
      p. cm.
   1. Seventh-Day Adventists. 2. Spiritual life—Seventh-Day Adventists. I. Title.
BX6154.K53 2011
248.4'86732—dc23
                                        2011019986

ISBN 978-0-8280-2521-8

Dedication

To all pastors, church leaders, and laypeople
who love God passionately
and want to do great things for the cause
of His kingdom and His church.

Acknowledgments

I am grateful to all my research assistants who worked tirelessly to make this book a reality. Kesia Reyne Bennett is a joy to work with. She added to the value of this manuscript in more ways than I can count.

I will forever hold a debt of gratitude to all the pastors, church leaders, and laypeople who were willing to be interviewed or completed our questionnaires so that others might benefit from the insights and experiences.

Contents

The Dream Church[1]

It is awesome.
  It is inspiring.
  It is all about love.
  It is a beautiful place.
  It is a seven-day church.
  I love this church so much.

These are the words used by people of growing Seventh-day Adventist churches to describe their congregations. They speak of their churches with love, passion, and enthusiasm. For them, church is an exciting place to do ministry and experience the grace of God in community.

God has a dream for your church. He desires that all members be able to say about their congregation what these people proclaim about theirs. The Lord desires it to be a vibrant community that influences lives for eternity and joyously serves Him in love. Imagine if everyone in your church were able to say:

  Here I feel safe.
  I am respected.
  I am growing in Jesus.
  I am involved in ministry.
  God is using me to touch the lives of others.
  I love my Sabbath school.

We have inspiring worship.

I am so proud of our church—I love inviting people to it.

I look forward to going to church. I could stay there all day.

I could never get tired of my pastor's sermons—they are filled with hope.

What happens at our church is a matter of eternal life and death. It's *that* important.

This is the experience of many who attend thriving Seventh-day Adventist churches in the North American Division. Loving God and their church, they are passionate about ministry, evangelism, and sharing Jesus with others.

Describing the Research

From 2003 to 2007 I and a small group of graduate research assistants undertook a project to study flourishing Seventh-day Adventist congregations in the North American Division (NAD). We were interested to know why some Adventist churches are growing and others are not. In our search for growing churches we contacted all the conferences within the NAD to identify those that had sustained 5 percent growth (in attendance, membership, and baptisms) for five consecutive years. We excluded those congregations ministering to highly receptive first-generation immigrant communities. Five churches met these criteria. Broadening our net to churches expanding at the rate of 3-5 percent for three to five years produced 18 more churches, bringing the total to 23.

In order to be able to compare the churches fairly, the researchers next located three congregations in the same geographical area that were either declining or in the plateau stage. Then we interviewed the pastors, one of the leaders, and three to five members from each church in the survey, asking them the following questions:

- What factors are contributing to the growth of your church? or What are the factors leading to the decline of your church or lack of growth?
- Do you have vision and mission statements?
- How often do you instill the vision in the heart of the congregation?
- How much time do you spend equipping, training, and motivating your members?
- Describe to us the atmosphere of your church.
- How do you feel about your worship service?
- What do you expect from the worship service?
- Is your church a safe place for its members?
- How inclined are you to invite someone to church?

• How many people did you invite to your church last year?
• How often do you share your faith?
• Do you have a strong prayer ministry?
• How many people in your church take prayer very seriously?

In addition, we conducted a survey on Sabbath morning to discover the devotional, ministry, and evangelistic practices of the active members. We will report much of the findings in this area in the section regarding active and committed laity.

In some ways we found ourselves encouraged by the practices of some of our members and the success of some of our churches, but our research made it clear that we have many challenges to growth. Most of our churches (more than 80 percent) are plateauing or in decline. In fact, the growth rate of the Seventh-day Adventist Church in the North American Division is going down. We are not even keeping up with the rate of increase in population.[2]

The Big Four

We discovered that church growth in the North American Division has a strong relationship to four major factors: effective and empowering leadership, passionate and authentic spirituality, committed and active laity, and God-exalting worship.

1. Empowering Servant Leadership

Growing churches have leaders—pastors, lay pastors, elders, or ministry directors—who genuinely want their congregation to grow and are willing to pay its cost. They are eager to work toward a changed culture, one evangelistic in nature, and are willing to shift from old methods to new and more effective ways of reaching people. As a result, they are not afraid to try new approaches and to invest the resources needed to ensure that the church is healthy. Such leaders tend to have a strong passion for the lost and an eagerness to do anything to connect them with the heavenly Father.

In interviewing the leaders of flourishing Seventh-day Adventist churches, it became clear that their leaders love evangelism—it is their holy preoccupation. Thus it takes only a few minutes of interaction with them to know that they are focused on reaching the lost. Not only do they model evangelism, but they inspire those around them to do the same. They have what I call evangelistic eyes—the ability to discern opportunities for sharing Jesus with others. As a result they find ways to witness in the supermarket or will join the gym to share Jesus. Perhaps they talk about God at birthday parties and bus stops. Always their hearts are filled with a compelling desire to share Jesus and make Him known.

Additionally, the leaders of thriving churches have strong, faith-based optimism that becomes the basis of their goals and actions. It informs their thinking so that they expect great things from God in prayer and labor, and they influence others to an optimistic outlook grounded in faith. Also they spend considerable time motivating and equipping others to do ministry and evangelism.

2. Passionate and Authentic Spirituality

Ironically, many people expressed the misconception that growing churches tend to de-emphasize spirituality, that they are more about showiness and superficial spirituality than about commitment and loving Jesus. The truth is that flourishing Adventist congregations tend instead to emphasize spirituality often, strongly, and passionately. Growing churches have a level of spirituality unmatched by the average congregation. We believe that it is this spirituality that is the source of passion and power behind their effectiveness.

3. Committed and Active Laity

No matter how effective pastors may be, they are still limited by time and competency. None are omnipresent or all-knowing, and none—no matter how they may try—can successfully pastor without rest and recreation. Fortunately, church growth is not about how active the pastor is in ministry and evangelism, but more about how active the members of the church are.

Our survey assessing the evangelistic practices of members across many types of Adventist churches (based on a random sampling of NAD congregations) revealed that the vast majority of them have not won one person to Jesus Christ during their lifetime. Not one. The data also demonstrated that our membership is aging and our congregations are struggling to attract new members and hold on to young ones. That same survey assessed the devotional habits of our congregations and told us that even our active members are weak in the practice of spiritual exercises such as reading the Bible and praying. But that is not the case in growing Seventh-day Adventist congregations. Their members are more spiritually involved and more evangelistic.

4. God-exalting Worship

Our research clearly demonstrates that the worship experience is a vital part of growing congregations. But contrary to the perception that such churches are contemporary in their method of worship, we discovered that the style is not essential. What is, however, is the quality of the worship experience, not its placement on the traditional-contemporary continuum. If the heart of the believer touches the heart of God, worship will take place. Though style is not mandatory for growth, excellence, and purpose, prayer, hope, and professionalism are vital.

So What's in Here?

The book you hold in your hands seeks to help your congregation transform into the church of your dreams and of God's vision for you. It is meant for anyone interested in advancing the kingdom of God, whether they be members, leaders, or pastors. The insights, ideas, tools, and techniques found here derive from the primary research just described, and we apply those findings in ways that any congregation can implement. Such flourishing churches can teach us to understand better the dynamics necessary for growing successful Adventist congregations. We have filled the book not with charts and statistics, but rather with stories of real people in real churches in real places making a real difference with real joy.

We build upon this primary data about thriving Seventh-day Adventist churches within the North American Division. Furthermore, the methods and principles outlined here not only are supported by empirical research but are in harmony with God's Word, the Bible. Sometimes we will use statements from the pen of Ellen G. White to shed additional light on key concepts. I have sprinkled throughout many personal stories from my own experience of the Lord's blessing of healthy growth in the congregations that I have pastored.

Let me make one more observation: though the research involved churches in the North American Division, the principles it reveals are universal and timeless. I did my best to present them in such a way that they will have worldwide applications. So whether you are from North America or South America, Africa or Asia, Europe or Australia, this book is for you. You can employ its principles in your own context.

We devote a section to each of the four major findings in our research: empowering servant leadership, passionate and authentic spirituality, committed and active laity, and God-exalting worship. The final chapter answers the question "Where to start?" by giving the first 10 steps toward your dream church. From beginning to end you'll find inspiring stories, startling research, and practical steps. The first chapter will deal with the biblical principles of church growth, church health, and evangelism.

The Heart of the Matter

This book operates on three assumptions:

1. Church growth involves cooperation between God and His people. God has entrusted to us a work that only He can do.

2. Church growth requires cooperation between believers and their congregation. They must be passionate about God to want to share Him, but they also must be proud of their church to have any desire to bring others to that community of faith. That is why I devote several chapters on

how to improve the atmosphere, worship service, and ministry of the local congregation. For consistent church growth members must want to be taught and trained for acceptable service, and thus the church must be a mini seminary to train and equip believers to fulfill their God-given gifts and potential.

3. Church growth is possible only through God's empowering presence. Let us connect with Jesus, who said, "Without Me, you can do nothing."

To pastors and elders, deacons and Sabbath school teachers, members of church boards, every ministry leader, and every member, I pray that this book will be a useful tool in your hand as you labor with God in His vineyard.

I love our church, and I'm passionate about our collective mission. I pray that this book will lead to a better way of doing church and create an urgency that seeks better connections with Christ, more dependence on the power of the Holy Spirit, more passionate prayer, and more vigorous ministry and evangelism that will produce meaningful change and renewal so that we might be more effective in fulfilling the mission of Jesus Christ.

---

[1] I am defining the dream church as a church that is living by the values of Jesus Christ outlined in Acts 2:42-47—a studying, worshipping, praising, fellowshipping, and praying church. It is a church filled with joy and unity and yet able to perform miracles. While a safe place to be, it is yet challenging enough to inspire people to do ministry and evangelism. Healthy and growing, it is filled with the Spirit and grace of God. Later on I will devote a whole chapter entitled "The Jesus-centered Life" to describing the spiritual elements and principles of such a church.

[2] David Beckworth and S. Joseph Kidder, "Refections on the Future of the Seventh-day Church in North America: Trends and Challenges," *Ministry*, December 2010, pp. 20-22.

The Biblical Foundation for Church Health and Growth

The Purpose of the Church

The church is in the world for three reasons. One of them—that of glorifying God's name—continues throughout time and eternity. To glorify the name of God in word and deed means nothing less than a total identification with and dedication to the purposes of the Creator, who calls us above all else to love Him with our whole being, and our neighbors as ourselves.

A second duty is to edify the body of Christ. This happens in many different ways, such as encouraging each other, praying for each other, loving each other, and training each other for evangelism and ministry. We are to contribute to the spiritual and evangelical growth of fellow believers and thus to be builders of a heavenly fellowship, bringing to this task whatever spiritual, intellectual, moral, and evangelistic possibilities are available to the biblically disciplined believer.

Extension of the kingdom is the third prong. God wants His church to grow and prosper. It takes place most effectively through those whose lives are God-glorifying and church-edifying. The church aims to equip all believers to function effectively as it influences and impacts the world for Jesus Christ. The risen Christ joins with His followers and, renewing them by the Spirit, invigorates them for witness and service in the world. The church can hardly glorify God's name or be truly edifying if it neglects its ambassadorial role of beseeching the lost to be reconciled to God. "As the Father has sent me, I am sending you," Jesus said (John 20:21).

This book deals with all these facets of the life of the church in one way or another. They are connected and feed into each other. A church that glorifies God will want to be intentional about edifying its members and training and equipping them for meaningful and effective ministry in the church and the world. Also such a church will be very deliberate about reaching the lost and leading them into the community of faith so that they will want to bring others with them.

This section of the book will deal with the biblical foundation of church growth, health, and evangelism. I will define all of these terms biblically and show how they work in the life of the believer and the church. Then I will deal with the power of God, which makes all things possible. The Lord has given us a task that only He can do. Thus it is imperative that we rely on His power and grace to be able to do the task ahead of us. I will conclude the chapter that follows with the motivation of believers as they are engaged in the work of evangelism and church growth and health.

Beyond question, church growth was a remarkable feature of first-century Christianity. No matter what happened to them, no matter what problem they faced, no matter what kind of persecution or opposition they endured, God continued to bless the church, and the growth of the fellowship of believers continued unimpeded—the church increased in grace and in numbers. If you and your church are faithful to God, if you live to glorify the name of Jesus and train your members for ministry, growth will also be a remarkable feature of your church in this century.

Chapter 1

What Does the Bible Say About Church Growth?

God wants His church to grow. Jesus said, "All authority in heaven and on earth has been given to me. Therefore go and make disciples of all nations, baptizing them in the name of the Father and of the Son and of the Holy Spirit, and teaching them to obey everything I have commanded you. And surely I am with you always, to the very end of the age" (Matt. 28:18-20). Any church concerned about growth and discipleship is really in touch with the heart of God and is doing what is pleasing to Him. His expressed will is that the good news of the gospel be communicated to all classes, all races, and all languages—in other words, to all people.

As the church obeys the Great Commission more intelligently, more effectively, and more fervently, the church will advance. And as Christians feel church growth responsibility, communicate the gospel, and educate those who are won to become responsible Christians themselves, congregations as a whole will receive the abundant blessing that God wants to give them.

Church growth takes place when the church is doing well spiritually. When it functions well, it is the hope of the world and source of change, new life, and the gateway to heaven. Each local congregation has a part in fulfilling the Great Commission. And each individual church is to bring love, hope, and joy to our sin-ridden and dying world.

The Definition of Church Growth

Church growth is teaching and training and modeling to the members to become what God desires them to be so that they can win people to the Lord Jesus Christ and His church. Thus church growth is a spiritual and yet practical conviction combining the eternal principles of God's Word with the practical insights of reaching the lost.

Growth of any kind follows a typical pattern. The local church has those who plant the seed (evangelists), those who water it (nurture/encourage/teach), and those who use their spiritual gifts for the further mat-

19

uration of members of the local congregation. But note that it is God who gives the increase (1 Cor. 3:7). Those who plant and those who water will each receive their own reward according to their labor (verse 8).

Acts 2:42-47 describes a thriving church in which the believers "devoted themselves to the apostles' teaching and to fellowship, to the breaking of bread and to prayer" (verse 42). They were serving one another and reaching out to those who needed to know the Lord, for God "added to their number daily those who were being saved" (verse 47). When these things are present, the church will experience spiritual growth, whether or not it results in actual numerical increase.

Church Growth in the Book of Acts

The book of Acts is the story of an unhindered gospel (cf. Acts 28:31). The whole book focuses on the remarkable growth of the church under the guidance of the Lord and through the power of the Holy Spirit. Luke punctuates his account with many summary statements about church expansion (Acts 2:43-47; 5:14; 6:7; 9:31; 12:24; 16:5; 19:20). We can find no better place to examine the factors that made the early church grow than the Acts of the Apostles.

Beyond question church growth was a remarkable feature of first-century Christianity. Acts clearly presents the gospel as—in the words of Paul—"the power of God that brings salvation to everyone who believes" (Rom. 1:16). It is able to overcome linguistic differences (Acts 6:7), conquer idolatry (Acts 12:22-24), and successfully face opposition (Acts 19:17-20). Luke most emphatically stressed the fact of church growth in his account of the development of early Christianity. No matter what you are facing in your congregation, the book of Acts is a great source of encouragement for all of us. Your church can grow if it is faithful to Jesus and lives to honor Him.

The Kinds of Church Growth

The first category is numerical growth. Luke named the 11 remaining apostles and described the believers in the first prayer meeting as numbering 120 (Acts 1:13-15). After the mighty movement of the Spirit on the day of Pentecost, those who accepted the message and were baptized totaled more than 3,000 (Acts 2:41). Often the gospel spread through entire families, villages, and towns (e.g., Acts 16:11-34). After the arrest of Peter and John in Jerusalem for preaching the good news of Christ, "many who heard the message believed; so the number of men who believed grew to about five thousand" (Acts 4:4). The book of Acts mentions other indications of expansion: "more and more men and women believed in the Lord and were added to their number" (Acts 5:14); "the number of disciples was increasing" (Acts 6:1); "the church throughout Judea, Galilee, and Samaria" "increased in numbers" (Acts 9:31). James and the other leaders of the Jerusalem church gave a remarkable testimony to such growth when they informed Paul "how many thousands of Jews . . . have believed" (Acts 21:20), not to mention the host of Gentile converts. Acts strongly underscores the fact of numerical increase. While Luke did not worship numbers, he certainly did not ignore them! In Acts the growth was *conversion* growth, for the church was just beginning its work in the world, and the Lord constantly added to its number (Acts 2:47).

The second kind is geographical growth. The gospel spread not only from one individual to another, but also from place to another. Acts records in broad terms the progress of the Christian message from Jerusalem to Rome and Athens (Acts 1:8; 9:15). The message of salvation moved out from its Jewish matrix into Samaria (Acts 8:5, 12), then farther into other areas, such as Phoenicia, Cyprus, and Antioch (Acts 11:19-26). The strong conviction that the gospel is for every person, race, nation, color, and language undergird the geographical expansion of the Christian message. Jesus Christ is relevant to the needs of the whole world, and therefore the whole world must receive an opportunity to hear the good news of "peace through Jesus Christ" (Acts 10:36). The missionary extension of the faith is no optional extra—it is in harmony with the gracious purpose of a loving God who does not want "anyone to perish, but everyone to come to repentance" (2 Peter 3:9).

The third type is spiritual growth. The early church's development was not simply quantitative but also qualitative. Besides an increase in numbers and in geographical outreach the new developing Christian communities throughout the world also experienced a definite deepening of spiritual life. An increase in godly living followed the preaching of the gospel.

The book of Acts faithfully records the spiritual growth of the early church. Acts 2:42-47 is a beautiful cameo of its inner life. (I will devote a whole chapter to this section of Scripture later on.) We see the spiritual maturation of the fellowship reflected in the boldness of the believers' prayer both in time of peace and in crisis (Acts 4:23-31). Also the voluntary, generous way in which Christians willingly shared their possessions showed the depth of the change that Christ was effecting in their lives (verses 32-37). The saintly way that Stephen died (Acts 7:59), the faithful manner in which Philip preached (Acts 8:4-40), and the courage of the early Christians in facing persecution (Acts 5:27-33, 40-42; 16:19-25) all bear witness to their growth in grace. Indeed, the leaders of the church paid attention to this nurturing process, "strengthening the disciples and encouraging them to remain true to the faith. 'We must go through many hardships to enter the kingdom of God'" (Acts 14:22; cf. 15:32, 35, 41; 18:23).

Luke presented a balanced picture of church growth that included numerical, geographical, and spiritual advancement. To him, the Christian faith was truly an evangelistic one, in which believers are to reach out to others and draw them to Jesus Christ. The Christian faith is also a missionary faith, attempting to cross national and cultural barriers to bring the gospel to every individual. And certainly Christianity is concerned with the edification and spiritual development of God's people. The biblical author's balanced picture of the early church gives careful attention to each of these factors. Church growth of any kind occurs best when the church is healthy and functioning well under the guidance of the Holy Spirit.

The Definition of a Healthy Church

A healthy church seeks to obey the Great Commission and Great Commandments in its setting by being biblically based, spiritually alive, mission-focused, functionally balanced, effective in its organization, servant-led, characterized by excellence in all that it does, and empowered by the Holy Spirit (Acts 2:42-47).

The key issue for churches in the twenty-first century will be church health, not church growth. When congregations are healthy, they advance the way that God intends. If your church is genuinely healthy, you won't have to worry about it growing. Thus the principles of this book that are intended to create a healthy church will naturally lead to development.

The Bible indicates seven signs of a healthy church. It (1) glorifies God; (2) produces disciples who seriously strive to obey the commandments of God; (3) has members that participate in ministry based on their spiritual gifts; (4) is incarnational—in the world and in the community, influencing them; (5) is active in evangelism; (6) assimilates new people into the life and leadership of the congregation; (7) trusts God and obeys Him in all things.

A healthy church is one in which every member grows, serves, witnesses, and builds up others. And all things that we do must come from the indwelling life of Christ in each believer's life (John 15:4, 5; Eph. 4:16). This is a profound paradigm transformation for many believers and churches. It is a shift away from a strategy to people and from program mentality to a Holy Spirit empowerment. If we can create a culture in which every believer takes responsibility to grow, serve, and witness in the power of God, our churches will transform their worlds!

Numerical growth constituted only part of the measure of the church. The deepening of relationships with God and with others must be part of a mature church. True church growth takes place when the local church supernaturally and faithfully fulfills the Great Commission in its unique context and with a vision for saving the world.

What Is Evangelism?

What feeds into the church and helps it to grow is what we call evangelism. The word "evangelism" does not appear in the New Testament, although the word "evangelist" occurs three times (Acts 21:8; Eph. 4:11; 2 Tim. 4:5). The evangelist is one who announces glad tidings or good news. Evangelism is both communicating the gospel so that a person understands it and persuading that individual to respond to the message.

At the heart of evangelism lies Jesus command to all His followers in all ages and places to "go therefore and make disciples of all the nations" (Matt. 28:19, 20, NKJV). Therefore, evangelism is an eagerness to win others for the kingdom of God by leading them to believe in Jesus Christ. It is bringing to someone the gospel of Jesus Christ, which is the realization that every human being is guilty of sin and in danger of being eternally lost; but because God loves us He sent His son to take our place and be the ultimate sacrifice for the sins of all humanity. He died on the cross, was buried and raised from the dead, and then ascended into heaven. All those who believe that Jesus is the Son of God and accept Him into their heart as their personal Savior and Lord will be saved and have eternal life.

Today the church employs diverse methods of evangelism to spread the gospel—public meetings, radio, television, satellite evangelism, etc. Yet the fact remains that a one-to-one approach initiated by every believer still is the most effective way of reaching the masses today. If in a single calendar year every Christian were to win one individual to Jesus, the multiplication of believers would far surpass anything yet reported in the modern missionary era. Evangelizing the lost in one's own neighborhood is at once the most natural and most strategic place to begin.

Knowing what evangelism is should lead us to do all ministries in a different light so as to make them evangelistic in nature. If your ministry is working with kids, it is not entertaining them or filling time—it is leading them to Jesus. Should you be an elder, it is not about reading Scripture on Sabbath morning or asking for the offering or making decisions for the congregation—your role is to disciple, encourage, pray, and lead the people to a deeper experience with God. Being a deacon is not just to collect the offering on Sabbath morning or open and close the doors of the church building, but to witness boldly for the risen Savior (see Acts 6:1-9). This principle applies to all ministries and to all those who confess the name of Jesus. Pray and dream of ways in which God can use you effectively and powerfully.

God's Empowering Spirit

The power for church growth is that of the Holy Spirit. The Holy Spirit calls people to faith. The power of God's Spirit is what helps them advance in discipleship. Whenever we find comprehensive church growth it is because the Holy Spirit has come afresh on His people.

The church was born on Pentecost (Acts 2:1ff.). From that time onward the apostles and followers of Jesus Christ displayed a new commitment, a new understanding, and a new vision of God's purposes. Now tuned in to God's plan, they had a new power, one that is part of the church until the Lord returns. The New Testament is the record of the church alive with the Spirit of God and not yet burdened by unproductive traditions and fruitless habits of faithless fear. The people of God went everywhere telling about Christ (Acts 8:14).

The Holy Spirit brings the church into being, sustains its inner life, renews it from time to time, empowers it for mission, and causes it to grow. We can readily see this from a careful study of the Acts of the Apostles, which is a manual on both the Holy Spirit and the church.

On the day of Pentecost, when the Holy Spirit was poured out in His fullness upon the early disciples, Peter, now empowered by the Holy Spirit, testified to and exhorted the crowd that had gathered, summoning them to repentance and faith in Jesus Christ. Three thousand of the crowd "accepted his message" and "were baptized" (Acts 2:37-41). Thus the church came into being. From that point onward we observe a close relationship between it and the Holy Spirit.

The Holy Spirit endowed the disciples with power for witnessing and preaching "and began to speak . . . as the Spirit enabled them" (verse 4). "And they were all filled with the Holy Spirit and spoke the word of God boldly. . . . With great power the apostles continued to testify to the resurrection of the Lord Jesus" (Acts 4:31-33). Christian congregations everywhere had a profound and overwhelming sense of the presence of the Holy Spirit.

The Holy Spirit called and commissioned the first missionaries in the church at Antioch. "While they were worshiping the Lord and fasting, the Holy Spirit said: 'Set apart for me Barnabas and Saul for the work to which I have called them.' So after they had fasted and prayed, they placed their hands on them and sent them off. The two of them, sent on their way by the Holy Spirit, went down to Seleucia" (Acts 13:2-4).

Furthermore, the Holy Spirit guided the missionaries, indicating to both where to go and where to avoid. The Spirit commanded Peter to visit the house of Cornelius at Caesarea (Acts 10). The Spirit ordered Phillip, the evangelist, to travel to Gaza (Acts 8:26-40). The Holy Spirit forbade Paul and Silas to enter Asia and Bithynia, but instead directed them to Macedonia (Acts 16:6, 7, 9, and 10). The Spirit led Paul to return to Jerusalem in spite of impending danger (Acts 20:22, 23).

In times of persecution the Holy Spirit comforted the church. "Walking in the fear of the Lord and in the comfort of the Holy Spirit, they were multiplied" (Acts 9:31, NKJV). The Holy Spirit guided the early church in matters of administration. Commenting on the momentous decision made at the first council in Jerusalem, Peter declared, "It seemed good to the Holy Spirit, and to us" (Acts 15:28, NKJV). When Paul admonished the elders of the Ephesian church, he reminded them that the Holy Spirit Himself had made them guardians of the flock (Acts 20:28). The Holy Spirit filled the church with God's presence, led the church, empowered it, and protected it.

The Motivation for Evangelism

1. Gratitude to Christ. Great hosts of first- and second-century Christians evangelized the world because of the overwhelming experience of the love of God that they had received through Jesus Christ. The discovery that the ultimate force in the universe was love, and that such love had stooped to the very depths of self-abasement for human good, had an effect on those who believed it that nothing could erase. Reflection upon the cross as the supreme example of costly service for others unquestionably kept the zeal of Christians at fever pitch. Gratitude to Christ is probably the greatest single theological factor in the believer's desire to grow congregations today. So proclaim the gospel and help create the kind of culture that enables people to experience the transforming grace and love of God. Those who have recently experienced this reality, for the first time or afresh, will be among your most motivated evangelizers.

2. Obedience to the Great Commission. Christ's summons to make disciples among all people is the banner pointing the way for the expansion of the church and its ministry and mission. The church exists as His body, extending His mission to all lost, hurting, and oppressed people. Thus the Great Commission is not a legal command that one obeys in some kind of Christian legalism. It is rather Christ's announcement of our identity. We accept the commission as an opportunity that permits us to join Him in the way that He leads. Churches that accept this offered privilege and have their priorities straight will experience apostolic growth.

3. Love for others. Lost people matter to God, and they must do so to us. Believers who compassionately want the lost found, the estranged reconciled, and the defeated empowered find themselves compelled to reach out to them. Rooted in agape love, such motivation has been prominent in every generation driven to do evangelization. The question that confronts each one of us is Do we have sorrow and grief for the lost? Do we care enough to reach out to them and share Jesus with them?

4. The conviction that Christ is with us. Christ is present in the world, and He is calling us to join Him as His ambassadors, through whom He can present His appeal. He promises to empower us—even to give us the words that fit particular circumstances. When the followers of the Savior become convinced that Christ Himself is leading and is with them, nothing can stop them. I frequently ask church leaders and members, "What are you now attempting in your evangelism and mission that would succeed only if God were with you?" Leaders and members of growing churches can hardly contain themselves about all the possibilities of what God can do in their midst. May this be your experience.

Healthy and Growing Seventh-day Adventist Churches

In the research we conducted regarding growing Adventist congregations, we discovered that those churches tend to be faithful to all the principles discussed in this chapter. If you want your church to be an expanding one, go back to the basics: learn how to pray and worship, learn to read the Bible and live by the ideal of Jesus, then learn to love one another and the lost. Build a culture that says that lost people matter to God. When you do that, you and your fellow members will have evangelistic visions that see opportunity to share Jesus everywhere you go and under all circumstances and situations.

God has promised that He both is the cornerstone and head of the church. May your congregation have that kind of solid foundation and leader, and may it be a light and a source of grace to your community and your world.

Section 2:

Empowering Servant Leadership

Everything in the church depends on leadership. It would therefore be wise to invest more in leadership training and development. Leaders not only set the stage and the tone for growth, but develop systems to help people to mature spiritually. Above all, leaders influence their congregations to serve God and people passionately.

This section has three chapters. They focus on:
1. Creating faith-based optimism
2. Redefining the spiritual leader: looking to Jesus
3. Being a leader maker

The first chapter builds upon the research that we did on the attitude of the pastors and leaders of growing Seventh-day Adventist churches. Though the interviews focused on clergy, the principles apply to all of us.

The second chapter is a biblical reflection on the role of the pastor and subsequently the leader. Thought it is not based strictly on the research that we did, we did discover that the leaders of the growing churches exhibit certain characteristics. It is essential for all pastors and members to understand the principles of this chapter. Pastors will then be free to do what God has called them to do, and the members will have the right expectations of their pastors. We will develop many of the principles presented in this chapter in more detail throughout the rest of the book.

The third chapter is about the importance of equipping, training, and liberating every member to do effective ministry and evangelism. It deals with some biblical principles, research, and personal stories taken from the churches that I pastored that experienced a phenomenal growth—one of them expanded from 40 people to about 500 in attendance.

The main role of every leader is to train and equip someone else to do the ministry they perform. I have been asking my students at the seminary if their local congregations have a systematic program of training and equipping. During the past 10 years only a handful have affirmed to me that their local church has any kind of training program for ministry and evangelism. Jesus spent three and a half years training people for ministry. Paul defines the role of the pastor as an equipper of the saints for the work of service to build up of the body of Christ.[*]

---

[*] Eph. 4:12; see also 2 Tim. 2:2: "And the things you have heard me say in the presence of many witnesses entrust to faithful people who will also be qualified to teach others."

Chapter 2

The Most Important Ingredient in Church Growth: Faith-based Optimism

"F aith" and "optimism" are two simple words that can change you, your church, and your future. A positive, healthy attitude based on hope and faith is the number one human ingredient in church growth. As mentioned previously, research done in the Adventist church from 2003 to 2007 identified the fastest growing congregations in North America (those with an increase of at least 5 percent in attendance, membership, and baptisms for five consecutive years).[1] In order to be able to compare the churches fairly, the study excluded all those churches ministering to highly receptive first-generation immigrant populations. Five churches met these strict criteria (named below as "Church A," "Church B," etc).[2] For each one of these fast-growing congregations, the researchers matched them with three churches in geographical proximity that were either declining or in the plateau stage.

Same Places, Different Results

At the time of our study, the fastest-growing congregation, Church A, was in mid-America. In order to understand the dynamic of this thriving church, the study interviewed three pastors of stagnant Adventist churches in the same area and asked them to explain what they saw as the reasons behind their lack of growth. Almost all of them said, "It is very difficult to work here. The people are not interested in the Adventist message. Most of them are Baptist or Charismatic." When I asked them, "What about the future?" they said, "It does not look good. The Baptists are getting stronger, and we are getting weaker."

Church A was a congregation planted in a medium-size city in the late 1990s and has a strong evangelistic ministry to the community. When interviewed about his city, the pastor of Church A said, "I love living here. The people of our city love God, we pray for them, we meet their needs, and they keep coming to our church. God has been so good to us. We started our church approximately eight years ago with a handful of people, and today we have more than 500 people in attendance."

Church B, situated in a Southern metropolitan area of more than 5 million people and close to downtown, experienced revitalization in the past decade or so. Currently it is a culturally diverse congregation with strong leadership and preaching, and with about 500 active attendees.

The pastors of plateauing or declining Adventist churches near Church B said that the people in the area were strong Baptists and not interested in the Adventist message. Surprised, I said, "Are you telling me that all of the 5 million people who live here are religious and churchgoers? After all, God has seekers everywhere, even in other denominations." I received no response.

In contrast, the pastor of Church B had a faith-based optimism. "We're not intimidated by challenges. Our role is to pray, to have effective ministries and evangelism, and God's role is to send the people to us."

Church C is a long-established church in a suburb of a populous city in the Pacific Northwest. The congregation has more than doubled its attendance to between 450 and 500. It operates a strong and innovative community service ministry. The pastor of Church C said, "The best thing that ever happened to me was to be here. The people in our area have no church connections or ties. We pray for them, we minister to their needs, and they come to our church."

But when we interviewed three pastors of declining congregations in that same area about the condition of their churches, they reported, "We live in one of the most secular places in the world, which makes it very difficult to do any kind of evangelism. People here do not think about God and they don't need Him, and they certainly don't need the church." One of those pastors commented that the percentage of people who go to church in Paris, France, is higher than the percentage who attend in his area. When they were asked about the future, the unanimous answer was, "It's going to become more difficult." Same place, much different attitudes, much different results.

And it's not just suburban or city churches that have opportunity to grow. Church D is in a small town in the central United States, but has been increasing well for its size (about 175 on Sabbath morning) and exercising various kinds of ministries in the community. The small-town setting did not deter its pastor. He believed that whether small town or big town, with faith in God the members of his church would be enthusiastic evangelists, praying for and inviting their friends. Accordingly, he worked to mature the church spiritually and make it a place worth inviting people to. Five years later the church had grown by 50 percent.

Church E, situated in a rural area in the West, had a strong community presence and a passion for growth. The attendance was around 400, predominantly Anglo-American. In addition, it also had a minority Hispanic constituency.[3] But it was not always so. At one time the church had been dying and the new pastor had arrived to hear words of discouragement: "This church will not grow. It's in a small town, and the town is not growing." Yet the pastor of Church E believed that God could grow that dying church, and with that faith he went forward, leading his church to become a bright light in their community and a dynamic, enthusiastic Adventist congregation.

The Most Important Ingredient

No single factor alone will help your church grow—including some imaginary, ideal location where numerical or other increase is automatic—and no combination of efforts or strategies will make your church develop without the Holy Spirit. But with the Holy Spirit we have every reason for optimism and enthusiasm for the future. Of the factors that our research study identified as contributing to church growth—including effective leadership, enthusiastic involvement of the members, utilizing the power of prayer, and inspiring and dynamic worship[4]—none was more important than faith-based optimism.

Winning Attitude

The most important ingredient in church growth is to have a winning attitude based on faith and trust in God. Attitude involves the way you perceive things—your views and how you interpret situations. In short, attitude is the mental filter through which a person sees the world. Some perceive the world through a filter of optimism, and no matter what happens, they always trust that God will make all things work for good for those who love Him (Rom. 8:28). We could define a winning attitude as one that does not result from what happens in the world, but how we decide to interpret events in the light of God's promises and activities in the world.

Attitudes can be either winning or defeating. Let me show you why we must reject a defeated attitude. God promised to give a land flowing with milk and honey to His people, but 10 of the spies that Moses sent out to explore it could not trust the Lord to fulfill His promise. They viewed things purely through human perception (see Num. 13:31). A defeated attitude hinders God's blessing and offends Him. The 10 spies had a foretaste of the land's goodness, but they didn't live to possess it because they mocked God and elicited His wrath upon themselves (Num. 14:20-23).

Moreover, a defeated attitude leads to anxiety and insecurity The spies left in confidence, with a spirit of adventure, but returned in fear, no longer trusting and relying on God (Deut. 1:28). The whole Israelite camp wept because 10 of the spies felt disappointed, betrayed, frustrated, and insecure, and they influenced everyone else to want to appoint a new leader to take them to Egypt (Num. 14:1-4) They ceased to trust in the Lord (Deut. 1:32, 33) A defeated attitude is the root of unbelief . It prompted the 10 spies to lose their faith in God and compare themselves to grasshoppers (Num. 13:33).

A winning attitude opens up your spiritual vision (verse 30). Joshua and Caleb had a different view of the situation. They were aware that the inhabitants were powerful and lived in large fortified cities. But they knew that God would keep His promise (Deut. 1:29-31). They expressed no fear at all. Rather they attempted to encourage the crowd.

"Joshua son of Nun and Caleb son of Jephunneh, who were among those who had explored the land, tore their clothes and said to the entire Israelite assembly, 'The land we passed through and explored is exceedingly good. If the Lord is pleased with us, he will lead us into that land, a land flowing with milk and honey, and will give it to us. Only do not rebel against the Lord. And do not be afraid of the people of the land, because we will devour them. Their protection is gone, but the Lord is with us. Do not be afraid of them'" (Num. 14:6-9).

A winning attitude is the mark of a godly leader. The Bible says that God was pleased with Joshua and Caleb (Deut. 1:35, 36). Joshua became Moses' successor. He led the Israelites into great victories on the battlefield. Leaders who trust God and believe in His ability to do the impossible will move their churches from where they are to where the Lord wants them to be.

Maintaining a Winning Attitude Regardless of Circumstances

I wondered why God wanted Moses to send spies to the land of Canaan. The Lord could have told Moses every little secret about the city and guided the children of Israel toward victory. But I have concluded that the Lord wanted to test their attitude. He allows us to go through circumstances before we can be actually blessed. How do we react to such issues? Do we feel anxious? Or do we trust in Him and His power?

An essential quality of a winning attitude is to respond with trust and confidence. Not only did the disobedient spies have a defeated attitude, but later on they sought to conquer the Promised Land in their own strength despite God's warning—and lost the battle (Num. 14:40-45). It is natural to feel nervous when we walk through hardships. We start reacting to situations by using our own strength, forgetting that God is in control of everything. When we meet strongholds standing in our way, we need to find strength in God. As we do, we will start to look beyond what we see in this world. The author of Proverbs declares that we must trust in the Lord with all our heart, shun evil, not lean on our own knowledge, and acknowledge the mighty one in everything that we do (Prov. 3:5, 6).

Attitudes are contagious. Is yours worth catching? Furthermore, attitudes are extremely powerful. Therefore attitudes of defeat have a disastrous influence on others. It is unbelievable how just 10 ordinary people turned almost all of Israel against Moses, Joshua, and Caleb. Sound familiar? One spoiled person in the congregation motivates the entire church to have a defeated mentality. Therefore I want to urge you never to give room to defeated attitudes in your life or your church. If I wanted to summarize this concept, I would say, Your attitude determines your destiny, your success, and your growth.

Winning the World for Jesus

When we say that people are not interested or are difficult to reach, we limit God, ourselves, and even those that we seek to influence. If you have the underlying belief that people are not interested, will you even try new methods or attempt anything at all?

The situation today is much the same as it was in the first century A.D. During it three major philosophical ideas represented by three major cities dominated much of thought. Jerusalem represented tradition, uninterested people, and rigidity in beliefs. Athens symbolized modern philosophy and openness to new ideas, and Rome stood for a culture of entertainment, hero worship, and hedonism. And in every city, faithful Christians faced unremitting persecution. Despite the challenges—challenges no easier than the ones we face today—the Christian gospel spread, and the kingdom of God grew. The first century is the era of church growth and Christian spirituality that we look back on with envy, but Christianity spread, not because it didn't have challenges, but because it had a strong faith in Jesus Christ and the power of His Spirit.

In our time God will again carry His church to triumph and success. If we want to be part of it, then we must believe in God and in His Spirit.

During the research interviews we heard many excuses about why individual congregations had failed to grow. One pastor said, "Our church is in a highly affluent area, and people have no need for God." Another one explained, "My church is in a very poor area, and thus people have to work two or three jobs to make ends meet—therefore they have no time for God or the church." Still another pastor told us, "My church is in a very educated part of town; people question God." A different one concluded, "My church is in a very rough part of town; people don't like to change, and it is difficult for them to come to our church." Yet another reasoned, "Because our church is in an extremely postmodern demographic, people are open-minded to everything except absolute truth." "My church is in an industrial part of town," its pastor suggested, "and people find it difficult to look at new ways of experiencing God."

We heard excuse after excuse after excuse for why churches were not growing. But the pastors of the growing churches have a faith that they can win the world for Jesus, and an attitude that says that all things are possible with God. They also have faith that with God every church could be growing, dynamic, healthy, and excited about ministry and evangelism. Such an attitude of hope tends to be contagious. The members of their congregations have the same faith, attitude, and optimism. As a result, they believe that God will do great things for them, their families, and their church.[5]

The Lord Is Willing to Do Great Things

We are coworkers with a God who can accomplish anything. "The Lord is willing to do great things for us. We shall not gain the victory through numbers, but through the full surrender of the soul to Jesus. We are to go forward in His strength, trusting in the mighty God of Israel."[6]

The Lord desires to do great things for His children and His church. Ellen White emphasizes that what God does does not depend on us. Faith-based optimism does not rest on wishful thinking or ignorance of reality. No, it is based on the power of God.

The Lord can do things that are impossible for us. Nothing is too difficult for Him—a reality that Scripture testifies to again and again. God gave a child to a barren woman who was 90 years old married to a man 100 years old (Gen. 17:17; 18:10-14); He gave a child to a virgin who never knew a man (Luke 1:34-38). He took a youth and defeated a giant (1 Sam. 17), and He promised that if we have the faith of a mustard seed we could move mountains (Matt. 17:20). The entire weight of the Scriptures is behind faith in a God who can do all things.

"Ah, Sovereign Lord, you have made the heavens and the earth by your great power and outstretched arm. Nothing is too hard for you. . . . You performed signs and wonders in Egypt and have continued them to this day, in Israel and among all mankind, and have gained the renown that is still yours. You brought your people Israel out of Egypt with signs and wonders, by a mighty hand and an outstretched arm and with great terror" (Jer. 32:17-21).

"Jesus looked at them and said, 'With man this is impossible, but not with God; all things are possible with God'" (Mark 10:27).

When people believe in the power of God, He rewards them with His rich and abundant blessings. The Lord is still almighty. Our optimism is based on His unchanging nature, His abundant power, His faithful promises.

The Faith Factor

How does an attitude of faith affect the church and make it grow?

1. Nothing is as inspiring as seeing God moving in our midst.

To witness God in action energizes individuals and congregations in an uncommon way. An attitude of faith enables Him to work miracles among us, and they beget more faith, which begets more of God's visible deeds.

2. We can choose our attitudes.

A winning attitude is more important than anything else—our past, our education, our bankroll, our successes or failures, fame or pain, whatever other people may think of us or say about us, our circumstances, or our position. It is more crucial than appearance, giftedness, or skill and will make or break a business, a church, or a home. The remarkable thing is that we have a choice every day regarding the attitude that we will embrace. We cannot alter our past or the fact that people will act in a certain way. Nor can we change the inevitable. The only thing we can do is choose our attitude.

3. An attitude of joy is contagious.

Joy in the Lord's work can permeate the whole congregation. Imagine your church as a joyous church, one energized with confidence in God and happy in His work.

What Kind of Leader Do You Want to Be?

What kind of leader do you want to be—full of excuses or full of faith and optimism? If you have the right kind of attitude you will be able to acquire the necessary skills for success, and God will give you the resources that you need. Someone might say, "You do not know my area. You do not know my church. You do not know the difficulties that I am facing, the conflicts that I have to cope with." Growing a church is not effortless, not even easy, but with God all things are possible, including expanding and maturing a congregation in a challenging area. The Lord has not called us to have the mentality of defeat, but rather the spirit of success. "For the Spirit God gave us does not make us timid, but gives us power, love and self-discipline" (2 Tim. 1:7). He has assured us that He will be with us always, even to the end of the age (Matt. 28:20).

The Price of Growth

We must be willing to grow and pay its cost. The cost of growth is that of changing the culture to believe in the God who can do the impossible. Faith will empower us to move from indifference to missional life, from tradition to transformation, from maintaining the status quo to engaging the present. An optimism based on God's promises enables us to move from ease and comfort to living with adventure, faith, criticism, and even pain; from putting in time to effectiveness; and from dead orthodoxy to living faith. We must move from our usual worship to touching the heart of God. From profession to passion. From plans to purpose. From pain to promise. From programs to people. And from paralysis to prayer.

Making It Happen: Four Practical Steps

1. Build your own faith first. Study God's action in the Bible and in history.

2. Live that faith. Demonstrate faith in word and action, always talking about the incredible power of God.

3. Instill a vision in the congregation of God's greatness through sermons, testimonies, slogans, banners, and songs.

4. Build an enthusiastic congregation with a healthy self-esteem that believes all things are possible.

- *Celebrate the blessings.* Call attention to the action of God in your church. Praise Him for high attendance and offerings. Make anniversaries a time to bless the past and mark how far the church has come. Have a time for prayers of thankfulness that focus on the good that God is doing in your congregation.
- *Change the language.* Address problems from the perspective of faith, calling them opportunities and challenges. Think of problems not as limitations but as occasions to be creative. Banish the word "failure" by blessing risk: "We are a church not afraid to try new things for God."
- *Recruit cheerleaders.* Find the people who have faith-based optimism and believe in limitless possibilities. Let them give testimonies, take leadership roles, and speak out at decision-making times.

Faith-based Optimism and You

Now the question is How does faith-based optimism affect us? You might say, "Well, I am not a pastor. I am just a regular member of my church and cannot do much." Faith-based optimism makes a difference in your life and witnessing in three ways.

1. It affects your perspective on God. Believing in faith-based optimism is to accept the reality that with God all things are possible, including His mandate to make disciples of all nations and people and tribes even if they are not receptive to start with.

2. It affects your witnessing and evangelism. Real growth in the church takes place when laypeople are passionate about the mission of Jesus Christ and are actively sharing His love with the world around them. Lack of member involvement in evangelism could be attributed to weak spirituality, failure of vision, fear of rejection, busyness, disdain of traditional methods of evangelism such as door to door and similar public methods, a professionalizing of evangelism, or doubt that people are interested in the gospel and particularly in our unique message. Some people may even be embarrassed by their local church. Others may not believe that whatever they say will make any difference in the world. But if you believe in the God who can do the impossible, you will be much more inclined to share your faith, believing that people will respond in a positive way.

You will recognize that God has His people everywhere, and many of them will be receptive to His calling. I often share my story of how I came to the Lord in one of the least likely cities in the world: Baghdad. If God found me on the streets of Baghdad, surely He has people everywhere and anywhere.

Faith-based optimism will also shape the *way that you do ministry*. Your ministry will have eternal significance. Whatever ministry you do— whether it is adult or children's Sabbath school, or whether you are a deacon or an elder—it is about leading people to the throne of grace, where their lives will be radically changed.

3. It affects your attitude about your church's ministry and its outreach. One of the greatest hindrances to God's work is that of our attitude. I cannot tell you how many times I have heard people say at church board meetings or elsewhere that a certain area is difficult to reach. "People here are not receptive. When we tried this before, it did not work. We do not have the money or resources to do this or that." But when you have faith-based optimism, you have new enthusiasm to share your faith, to try something different to reach people, to adapt old methods to fit the new time and generations. Your church will be become a place of hope and faith and growth. Faith-based optimism becomes a reality when all leaders and members buy into it and it permeates throughout the entire life of the church from song service to ministry, and from committee meeting to evangelism.

Faith-based Optimism

An attitude of optimism and faith means that instead of letting challenges intimidate us, we expect God's triumphant intervention. We pray for conversions in large numbers as we work in the power of the Holy Spirit. And we anticipate that God will do great things.

What are your expectations? God will reward you according to your faith and what you look forward to. Therefore, wait and pray for great worship, great services, great faith, great Sabbath school, great people, and great growth. Expect God to do great things. Expect God to help you fulfill your potential. Expect people to be transformed and to change the world and to do wondrous things for God.

Moses sent 12 men to check out if it was possible to take the Promised Land. Ten men come back and claimed that it was impossible. But two men said that if God is with us, we can do it.

How about it, my friends? Join me in believing that with God on our side marvelous things will happen, our churches will be exciting places to be, and we can win the world for Jesus Christ.

"Prayer and faith will do what no power upon earth can accomplish. We need not be so anxious and troubled. The human agent cannot go everywhere, and do everything that needs to be done. Often imperfections manifest themselves in the work, but if we show unwavering trust in God, not depending upon the ability or talent of men, the truth will advance. Let us place all things in God's hands, leaving Him to do the work in His own way, according to His own will, through whomsoever He may choose. Those who seem to be weak God will use, if they are humble. Human wisdom, unless daily controlled by the Holy Spirit, will prove foolishness. We must have more faith and trust in God. He will carry work out with success. Earnest prayer and faith will do for us what our own devising cannot do."[7]

---

[1] To find such congregations, the researchers contacted every local conference in the North American Division and asked for the names of churches within their jurisdiction that met the criteria of the study. Once the study had identified the growing congregations (as well the plateaued churches in close geographical proximity), it interviewed the pastors about what they felt made their churches grow, about training and equipping the members, about prayer in their churches, and about worship in their churches.

[2] Using the broader criteria of 3 to 5 percent growth for three to five years led to a total of 23 churches. This chapter, however, relates the characteristics of the top five fastest-growing churches, all of which had at least 5 percent growth for at least five years.

[3] The Hispanic element was not included in the growth calculations, but was in addition to it.

[4] Our research indicated that there was no one style of worship associated with church growth.

[5] "The pastor's response will set the tone for the congregational response. If the pastor publicly appears defeated, bitter, disappointed, or depressed, the congregation will mirror his feelings" (Howard K. Batson, *Common-Sense Church Growth* [Macon, Ga.: Smith & Helwys, 1999], p. 89).

[6] Ellen G. White, *Sons and Daughters of God* (Hagerstown, Md.: Review and Herald Pub. Assn., 1955), p. 279.

[7] Ellen G. White, *Manuscript Releases* (Silver Spring, Md.: E. G. White Estate, 1990), vol. 8, p. 218.

Chapter 3

Redefining the Biblical Role
of the Spiritual Leader:
Looking to Jesus

When I graduated from the seminary and went to my first church, I asked several seasoned pastors various questions: "What is my role as a pastor? What I am supposed to be doing?" One said, "Just go out there and make the people happy." Another encouraged me to visit, visit, and visit some more. Yet another one felt that the main role of the pastor is to bring new people to the church. It led me to a study on the role of the spiritual leader that lasted for several years.

Pastors and other spiritual leaders carry with them the weight of many expectations, both those that originate from their congregations and those from their own sense of duty. People assume that pastors will be administrators, counselors, visionaries, preachers, teachers, answering services, and directories. Often they find themselves pulled in many different directions, always busy but never sure if they are pursuing their calling or chasing rabbits. Understanding the biblical role of the spiritual leader can free the pastor to focus on the right things and help the members to have the right expectation of them. It will lead to harmony in the church, and witnessing, evangelism, and discipleship will be front and center. After all, is that not what God has called us to do?

The Bible study that we are about to begin (on the role of the pastor) will establish some indispensable principles for church health and growth. What we found in our research is that the pastors or the spiritual leaders of growing churches focus on these vital principles and live them in their ministry. Also we discovered that the members of thriving churches tend to have the proper expectation of their ministers. A proper grasp of the biblical role of the pastor is crucial. The reason so many of our churches are not growing is that pastors are doing everything except what God has called them to do.

According to Scripture, what is their biblical function? Do we have a model in the Bible that might help us understand their proper role?

After many years of observation and careful examination of the literature,[1] it seems to me that there exist two distinct approaches to the pastorate: the traditional and the contemporary.

The Traditional Role

For many centuries people viewed the role of the pastor as a servant-caregiver who performs a series of separate acts, such as:

(1) teaching and preaching of doctrine

(2) caregiving (visitation, counseling, comforting, meeting the needs of people, etc.) performing rites of passages (baptisms, weddings, and funerals)

(4) administration (such as overseeing meetings, putting together a bulletin, coming up with some programs for the church, and hopefully reaching out to the community through some sort of evangelism)

(5) acting as the ambassador of the church to the community

But around the 1970s and 1980s a new understanding began to emerge. Many books and pastors of megachurches started promoting the role of the pastor as a CEO, a leader who casts a vision and rallies and motivates people to carry it out in a changed and healthy environment.

The Contemporary Role

Most books on church growth and leadership today argue that if pastors continue to do what they have done for so many years, they are dead in the water. Greg Ogden, in *Unfinished Business,*[2] proposes that the pastor should be a visionary leader who is constantly fostering other leaders, casting the vision, and changing the culture as well as the structure—and doing all of this with an eye for mission, evangelism, and church growth. I found such ideas to be fresh, insightful, and useful. However, they often do not have much theological undergirding that ties them together.

The old model of a servant-caregiver does not lend itself to growth. It creates a culture of people dependent upon the pastor to meet their needs and those of others. Utterly inconsistent with the biblical principles of the priesthood of all believers, it encourages believers to focus on themselves and thus hinders the growth of the kingdom of God.

The new model of a CEO leader is a mixture of biblical insights and business practices. Most of the church growth books present leadership models adapted to the context of the church. The approach has many potential dangers. First, it might lead people to follow a charismatic personality rather than biblical principles. Second, the new model focuses on the local congregation to the exclusion of the global church. It can lead to an emphasis on the building of a megachurch rather than creating a healthy church. Finally, any model we adapt needs biblical and theological development. I believe very strongly that the role of the pastor should derive from a biblical model and have a strong theological foundation.

The Biblical Role of the Pastor

So what is the biblical role? What are pastors supposed to do? For that matter, what does the Bible say about all committed disciples of Christ—the priesthood of all believers?

I think we will find our answer through studying the ministry of Jesus. He modeled to us how the ideal pastor lives and what the ideal pastor does. As we examine the life and ministry of Jesus, we discover that when He was here on earth He did five things: Jesus built His relationship with His Father, He preached the gospel of the kingdom of God, He met the needs of people, He made disciples through the power of the Spirit, and He gave His life as a sacrifice.

This is, in essence, what the pastor should do. Pastors must emulate their ideal model, Jesus Christ. And when they do that, then they are discipling members who then disciple still others so that the church becomes dynamic and growing with the Holy Spirit working in all members.

Let's unpack these five thoughts to develop a clear theological understanding of ministry for us today.

The first significant thing that Jesus did was to maintain a close relationship with the Father. Repeatedly Scripture shows us that Jesus placed the highest priority of His life on spending time alone with the Father. His life reveals an intense passion for God's presence as His heart longed and hungered to touch the heart of God. Note the following incidents in His life:

"It was at this time that He went off to the mountain to pray, and He spent the whole night in prayer" (Luke 6:12, NASB).

"After He had sent the crowds away, He went up on the mountain by Himself to pray; and when it was evening, He was there alone" (Matt. 14:23, NASB).

"In the early morning, while it was still dark, Jesus got up, left the house, and went away to a secluded place, and was praying there" (Mark 1:35, NASB).

Jesus lived a life of prayer. He started every day in communion with the heavenly Father and ended it in close relationship with His Father. At times He even spent the whole night in communion with His Father. Actually, Jesus was in touch with His heavenly Father all the time.

The very first thing that Jesus did each day was to fill the well of His being with the presence of His Father. He then lived with heaven in mind all day long. Jesus managed His time by moving from being to behaving. His being was about being in union with the Father and experiencing the joy of His Sonship. And His doing was that of performing the will of the Father. It is what made His every action so effective. Through His communion He received grace and power from the Father.

Emphasizing the need for us to do the same, Ellen White, in her book *Steps to Christ*, said, "His humanity made prayer a necessity and a privilege. He found comfort and joy in communion with His Father. And if the Savior of men, the Son of God, felt the need of prayer, how much more should feeble, sinful mortals feel the necessity of fervent, constant prayer."[3]

In the same book she also admonishes us to start every day with prayer. "Consecrate yourself to God in the morning; make this your very first work. Let your prayer be, 'Take me, O Lord, as wholly Thine. I lay all my plans at Thy feet. Use me today in Thy service. Abide with me, and let all my work be wrought in Thee.' This is a daily matter. Each morning consecrate yourself to God for that day. Surrender all your plans to Him, to be carried out or given up as His providence shall indicate. Thus day by day you may be giving your life into the hands of God, and thus your life will be molded more and more after the life of Christ."[4]

Scripture tells us that Jesus lived a life of complete connectedness to the heavenly Father. It's clear from the texts that Jesus prayed in the morning, in the evening, all night, and before and after crises. He was effective in ministry because of His prayer life. Joy filled His life because of it. It connected Him with the Father and enabled Him to have constant communion with the Father. Because of His commitment to prayer, Jesus carved out daily time in His crowded schedule for prayer. No one was busier than Jesus. The fate of the whole world rested on His shoulders, yet He always found much time for communion with God. His example is what we must have today. The church desperately needs to emulate Jesus' way of doing ministry.

I believe that it is no coincidence that Jesus instructed His disciples to prioritize their relationship with God before they went about preaching the gospel to Jerusalem, Judea, Samaria, and the ends of the earth (see Acts 1:4, 5).

The issue of prayer is so important that Jesus went as far as to declare that without our connectedness with Him we can do nothing. "If you remain in me and I in you, you will bear much fruit; apart from me you can do nothing" (John 15:5).

The work of ministry is first and foremost a summons to know the Lord Jesus Christ intimately and passionately. Our Savior calls us from loneliness to solitude, from depending upon ourselves to relying on Him. Jesus said to

His disciples and to us, "Come away by yourselves to a secluded place and rest a while" (Mark 6:31, NASB). As A. W. Tozer put it: "We are called to an everlasting preoccupation with God."[5] The heart of pastoral work is a spiritual one of connecting with God and helping others to do the same.

The second significant thing that Jesus did while here on earth was to preach the gospel. Jesus constantly proclaimed a message of God's love for them. In describing His earthly mission, Jesus said, "The Spirit of the Lord is on me, because he has anointed me to proclaim good news to the poor" (Luke 4:18). Also, Matthew 9:35 reminds us, "Jesus was going through all the cities and villages, teaching in . . . synagogues, and proclaiming the gospel of the kingdom" (NASB).

Jesus taught the people every day, giving guidance through the Word and calling them to confess their sins and to experience a transformed life.

The ministry of the Word always leads people to changed and transformed lives. The Word has power. The Word of God brought our world into existence and summoned Jesus Christ from the grave. And it is the Word that brings us back to spiritual health and vitality and produces meaningful change and transformation.

From an early age Jesus developed a passionate love for Scripture. He learned it and taught it with power and authority (Luke 2:46-50). His love for the Father motivated Him to read His book and learn about His will.

The pastor should always lead people to a better understanding and living of the Word of God. Notice the following vital spiritual things that the Word does for us.

God's Word gives us life (Phil. 2:16).

God's Word can make us righteous (1 Cor. 15:1, 2).

God's Word can produce growth (1 Peter 2:2).

God's Word sanctifies us (John 17:17).

God's Word gives us wisdom (Ps. 119:98).

I am afraid that many times we reduce Scripture to mere information. Paul reminds us that it is to give us a new life in Jesus by correcting our behaviour and actions. The apostle urged Timothy to give careful attention to the public reading and preaching (expounding) of the Scriptures (see 1 Tim. 4:13). He reminds Timothy that the whole of Scripture is divinely inspired and therefore "profitable for doctrine, for reproof, for correction, for instruction in righteousness" (2 Tim. 3:16, NKJV).

Ellen White makes it clear that we need to study the Scriptures not for knowledge, but for transformation:

"It is not theoretical knowledge you need so much as spiritual regeneration. You need not to have your curiosity satisfied, but to have a new heart. You must receive a new life from above before you can appreciate heavenly things."[7]

Thus it's time to stop rehearsing what we believe and instead to start looking at what difference it makes. We do not need knowledge so much as spiritual renewal. Let us study the Bible not from the pursuit of intellec-

The Essence of Pastoral Ministry

We find the essence of pastoral ministry embedded in Mark 3:13-15. "And He went up on the mountain and summoned those whom He Himself wanted, and they came to Him. And He appointed twelve so that they would be with Him and that He could send them out to preach and to have authority to cast out the demons" (NASB).

The passage contains three truths:

1. Jesus summons us to be with Him. Ministry does not start by being with people. Rather, for it to be effective and lasting it must begin with being in the presence of God. A few years ago Fuller Theological Seminary did a study on the devotional life of pastors and discovered that the average minister in the United States spends about five to seven minutes in prayer every day, while the effective pastor devotes at least an hour. God asks us to invest our lives with Him, to walk and talk and do ministry and evangelism totally dependent on the Holy Spirit and the power of God.

2. He sends us out to preach and heal and make a difference in the world. I have realized that a Christ-honoring, authentic Christian life is a prerequisite to having a compassionate heart toward the lost. Effective pastoral ministry does not start with the masses, but with much time alone with the Father. The more time we spend with God, the more successful our life will be. Many pastors are spiritually running on empty because they spend much of their time doing ministry and not letting God do His ministry to them. Fill up the heart with the presence and the anointing of the Spirit of God, and your ministry will have the signature of heaven stamped all over it.

3. We do all that through the power of the Holy Spirit. If you want to have the power of the Holy Spirit in your life and ministry, live connected with the Father. The secret of all success in ministry is our suc-

tual knowledge but to have a new heart. That is the essence of the power of the Word. Jesus did not preach sociology, politics, or even His own ideas—He always preached the Word. That is why He had power and authority. By the hundreds and thousands people came to Him because He offered the Word of God to them.

cess in secret prayer. We can do more than pray—after we have prayed. But we can never do more than pray until we have first prayed.

Ellen White presents it so strongly: "The reason why our preachers accomplish so little is that they do not walk with God. He is a day's journey from most of them."* She does not say that our pastors are not effective because they do not know enough theology or have not mastered enough strategies of church growth or even that they could be better preachers or ministers. Rather, she explains that they are not effective because they have not walked with God. He is a day's journey away from most of them.

A friend of mine commented to me few months ago, "Joe, I have been struggling to know why it took Peter one sermon to bring 3,000 people to the Lord, but now it is taking me 3,000 sermons to bring one soul to the Lord. Well, recently the Lord showed me why. It is the difference of doing ministry depending on Him or depending on our strength." My prayer is that all of us will do ministry and evangelism in the power and effectiveness of God.

When the pastor lives a life of prayer like that of Jesus, and becomes intentional about discipleship and spirituality, God will use him or her to transform the church into a sanctuary for spiritually transformed lives. Jesus announced, "My house shall be called a house of prayer" (Matt. 21:13, NASB). He did not state that His church should be a place of singing or preaching or doing ministry, though such things are important. Instead, the church is fundamentally the place for leading people to experience the presence of God and receive power from Him. Unfortunately, too many technicians have invaded the church with their programs and ideas and turned it into a human institution rather than the living body of Christ. When we live a life of connectedness with the heavenly Father, the church becomes a sanctuary of prayer, grace, and the indwelling of the presence of God. Jesus' hunger for the presence of God should be our own motivation and inspire us to be more and more like Him.

---

*Ellen G. White, *Testimonies for the Church* (Mountain View, Calif.: Pacific Press, 1948), vol. 1, p. 434.

We find the ministry of the Word of God expressed in a number of evangelistic sermons recorded in the book of Acts. But it is apparent that preaching and exhortation also took place when Christians gathered for worship and for the celebration of the Lord's Supper (see Acts 20:6ff.). The needs of evangelism and education, as well as edification, made it essential that the ministry of the Word be included as an integral part of the ministry of the church. The apostles were called to the ministry of the Word (Acts 6:2). Church leaders were to be able teachers of the Word of God (1 Tim. 3:2).

As I learned more about the importance of the Word of God, my approach to doing ministry changed. I started to put much more emphasis on Scripture than I ever had done before. In the past the Word of God had been about doctrine, knowledge about God, and the source of sermon ideas. Now it became the source of power and transformation and change. Developing an intense passion for the Word, I stared to teach it with greater clarity and effectiveness. Soon I noticed that something in me had started to change.

One of the things I began to do when I read the Bible was to ask the question "What is it in my life that needs change, or transformation, or encouragement?" For example, with the story of Jonah, I asked myself, "In what way am I showing rebellion toward God? Or in what way am I running away from Him? Do I love lost people as much as He does?" Such questions revolutionized my Scripture reading and my life. When I taught these principles to my congregation, I saw the same thing happening to them. In our journey with God together we moved from knowledge to power, from knowing the text to knowing God, and from mastering the text to God mastering us and transforming us.

The third significant thing that Jesus did was to meet the needs of people. More than once the Bible says that "seeing the people, [Jesus] felt compassion for them, because they were distressed and dispirited like sheep without a shepherd" (Matt. 9:36, NASB). Jesus loved people. He knew that lost people matter to God, and therefore they mattered to Him.

Ellen White, in *The Ministry of Healing*, outlines Christ's method of winning people.

"Christ's method alone will give true success in reaching the people. The Savior mingled with men as one who desired their good. He showed His sympathy for them, ministered to their needs, and won their confidence. Then He bade them, 'Follow Me.'"[7]

Jesus set out to build relationships and meet needs. The first thing He did was to associate with people from a desire to help them. By doing so, He touched their hearts. Second, He demonstrated His sympathy for them by manifesting an interest in their secular affairs. In another place White wrote, "Let them see that our religion does not make us unsympathetic or exacting."[8] The third thing Jesus did was to gain their confidence. Not until we have first built a relationship with others, met their needs, and touched their hearts, can we bid people to follow Jesus.

Notice the progressive steps that Christ took in witnessing, which shows us how we can, through an intimate relationship with Him, follow the same pattern to bring love, power, and compassion to those around us.[9]

1. Christ associated with others and sought their good.
2. He sympathized with them.
3. He ministered to their needs.
4. He won their confidence.
5. He invited them to follow Him.

Meeting the needs of the people was the essence of the early church and took many forms and expressions. In Acts 3:1-10 we find Peter healing a crippled man and in Acts 9:32-36 another paralytic who had been bedridden for eight years. Continuing in the same chapter, we learn about Dorcas, who started the first community service center. Not only did she and her helpers have a fully functioning community service program to provide food and clothes to the needy but miracles of healing and transformation accompanied their efforts. The book of Acts reveals that the early Christians aided not only each other but also the people in their communities.

Often as Christians we might be tempted to remove ourselves from this world, when in reality what we must do is not only be in this world (though not of it) but to socialize, build relationships, and win confidence. "We are not to renounce social communion. We should not seclude ourselves from others. In order to reach all classes, we must meet them where they are."[10]

One day I went to the largest grocery store in town. Stationing myself at the entrance, I asked about 20 people as they left the store if they knew where the local Seventh-day Adventist church was. Not one individual was able to tell me. As the pastor of that invisible church, I took this as a matter of prayer. When I shared my finding with the church board, we all felt the need to be much more intentional about doing things in our community. We decided that such involvement should be on a personal level as well as on a corporate level. I joined some civil organizations, and so did some of my members. Our church got involved in building homes for poor people, as well as conducting seminars on parenting and cooking. In addition, we opened our gym for community youth activities and our facility for Alcoholics Anonymous and literacy classes. As a result, we became very well known in the community.

Eight years later, when a new Adventist pastor from a neighboring church visited, I shared with him the story of standing at the door of the grocery store and asking the people if they knew where the Adventist church was. He decided to do the same. Waiting at the entrance of the largest grocery store in his town, he raised the same question. Almost all the people he stopped told him that while they did not know where the Adventist church was in his town, they did know where it was in our town. We need to ask ourselves, "If our church should suddenly vanish, would people miss us?"

A fourth significant thing that Jesus did was to make disciples through the Spirit. As soon as He began His public ministry at the age of 30, Jesus began to call people to be His disciples. He empowered 12 men to be His disciples, 12 men who would champion His evangelistic cause. As Robert Coleman says in his book *The Master Plan of Evangelism:* "His concern was not with programs to reach the multitudes, but with men whom the multitudes would follow. . . . Men were to be His method of winning the world to God."[11] Jesus defined teaching as training for a way of life, not as transferring information from one mind to another.[12] His teaching ministry was more about building new people for a new way of life.

He concentrated upon those He intended to use to transform the world, not on programs and not on the masses. It was always His methodology. That is why Jesus challenged His disciples by saying, "The harvest is plentiful, but the workers are few. Ask the Lord of the harvest, therefore, to send out workers into his harvest field" (Luke 10:2).

Jesus basically says that we have a math problem on our hands. We need more workers—more disciples—to gather the harvest, so we must go and make disciples of all nations. Our role is to pray for the harvest and especially for harvesters. God's role is to send us people who will be the new harvesters.

The need to build disciples is so fundamental that Jesus spent three and a half years in full-time discipleship formation. In fact, if He had not done so, the church would not exist today. And if we do not form the new generation of leaders, there will be no church in the future.

The New Testament church followed in the footsteps of Jesus. Not only did they baptize new believers daily through their Spirit-filled witnessing and preaching, but they were intentional in raising a new generation of leaders. Acts 6 indicates that the apostles selected and called others as disciples to help them do ministry and leadership in the church and in the world. Soon they also began to understand, practice, and preach the priesthood of all believers. Peter declared, "But you are a chosen race, a royal priesthood, a holy nation, a people for God's possession, so that you may proclaim the excellencies of Him who has called you out of darkness into His marvelous light" (1 Peter 2:9, NASB). Everyone was considered to be a disciple and had a ministry to perform. Again we must remember that much of what we are saying about the minister applies to all followers of Christ who seek to grow and to minister to others.

Paul was in the habit of having an apprentice. He started early on, taking Barnabas with him. Then we see him mentoring John Mark. But one of the most powerful examples was that of Timothy. The apostle invested his life to train, equip, motivate, and inspire the young pastor. What is so interesting is that Paul urged Timothy to do the same to others. In 2 Timothy 2:2 he wrote, "And the things you have heard me say in the presence of many witnesses entrust to reliable people who will also be qualified to teach others."

The question has often risen, "How do you find new leaders in the church?" My answer is to pray about it and claim God's promise. One of the most neglected promises in Scripture about leadership is that found in Matthew 9:35-38:

"Jesus went through all the towns and villages, teaching in their synagogues, proclaiming the good news of the kingdom and healing every disease and sickness. When he saw the crowds, he had compassion on them, because they were harassed and helpless, like sheep without a shepherd. Then he said to his disciples, 'The harvest is plentiful but the workers are few. *Ask the Lord of the harvest, therefore, to send out workers into his harvest field.*'"

Christ's method of selecting leaders was prayer. Lost people, needy people, hurting people, sick people surround us, but we have few seeking to reach them. We need to pray so that God will send us the right individuals to work with various groups of people and needs. The traditional way of finding leaders is to take whoever is willing or outspoken or can be talked into it. But God wants us to pray that He Himself will lead us to His choice, someone who is filled with the Spirit of God and with wisdom, and has the favor of people. God's choice will come with His passion to minister, and He will birth in their hearts the ministry they are wired for and are gifted to do.

Jesus demonstrated this model to us when He selected the apostles. He spent the whole night in prayer beforehand so that God the Father would lead Him to the right people.

"One of those days Jesus went out to a mountainside to pray, and spent the night praying to God. When morning came, he called his disciples to him and chose twelve of them, whom he also designated apostles: Simon (whom he named Peter), his brother Andrew, James, John, Philip, Bartholomew, Matthew, Thomas, James son of Alphaeus, Simon who was called the Zealot, Judas son of James, and Judas Iscariot, who became a traitor" (Luke 6:12-16).

One of the churches that I pastored desperately needed a youth pastor. The congregational leadership sent me to the conference armed with many charts and statistics to persuade them to send us a youth pastor. But because of lack of funds, they were not able to fulfill our request. A few days later, as I was having my devotions, I came across Matthew 9, and for the first time it hit me: finding new leaders in the church is about serious prayer and pleading with God. So I started to pray and got the church to pray and claim the promise in Matthew. About four months later I received a call from one of our students who was attending Walla Walla University and preparing for the ministry. The young man asked to meet with me that weekend.

The next Sunday we met in a restaurant, and after a pleasant meal he said to me that he had been thinking seriously about coming back home for a year to build our youth ministry. He ended up giving two years of his life to build a fantastic youth ministry and made sure that they would have strong leaders to carry the torch after him. Through this experience I saw vividly how this promise really works.

The experience was so powerful that it shaped the way that we did business in our church. Our ministry placement committee became a prayer meeting, and our leadership and board meetings became opportunities to pray and seek God's direction, wisdom, and leaders.

Another question I am frequently asked is about the best way to train people in the church. My answer is "on the job." The pastor should create a whole culture of equipping, training, motivation, and accountability. Every leader should be building a new leader. Fostering the new generation of leaders fulfills the mandate of Jesus to equip the new believers for effective ministry and evangelism.

Moreover, if a church is not intentional about raising the new generation of leaders, it will not have any increase in attendance. There might be growth on the books, but not in the number of people who actually attend. It is effective leaders who meet the needs of others. They are the ones who bring people to the church, minister to them, and keep them in the church.

As I learned about such things, I started to create a system to keep continually raising new leaders. Every one of our leaders, in whatever ministry he or she was, were supposed to train, mentor, and motivate another one to carry on in that area.

To lead and model this value, I prayed that God would send me someone that I could train. The Lord put a particular name on my heart. I approached John and cast the vision that God had given me to prepare new leaders. He told me that he had been praying for someone to mentor him in spirituality and ministry. We agreed to go out on Mondays from 6:00 to 9:00 p.m. and give Bible studies, since this was his passion. Our driving time was an opportunity to share with him what God had put in my heart. Every Monday we spent three to four hours together praying and conducting Bible studies. I especially emphasized the importance for him to mentor someone else as I mentored him.

About three months later I felt that he was ready to carry the torch himself. So I told him to take Ted with him, and I would take Glen with me. Glen was more interested in hospital visits, so every Monday we went to hospitals, nursing homes, and shut-ins.

Seven and a half years later we had 57 teams going out every night of the week to do all kinds of ministry. We probably trained more than 150 teams, but not all stuck with it. But, praise the Lord, now we have hundreds of people performing ministry every night of the week—something that is impossible for one person to do. Not only that, but we fulfilled the mandate of the New Testament to raise and equip the new generation of leaders. Every member should be seeking both to be discipled and to disciple. The grace of God will enable every member to do all the things that we listed in this chapter and not just delegate it to the professional ministers.

Build that system everywhere in your church. Your members will grow in love and in ministry. And your church will grow in grace and in numbers.

Finally, the fifth thing that Jesus did while here on earth was to give His life in service and in sacrifice. The life of Christ displays two important truths. First, He was a servant leader. Any study of Christian leadership is incomplete if we ignore the servant-sacrificial life of Christ. It is essential to recognize at the outset that He epitomized the concept of servant leadership by His own statement: "The Son of Man did not come to be served, but to serve" (Mark 10:45). "I am among you as one who serves" (Luke 22:27). The king of the whole universe was not into self-glorification, self-satisfaction, power, or control. Rather, His motivation was service and ministry.

The second truth about Jesus is that He gave His life as a living sacrifice. The Bible says, "For God so loved the world that he gave his one and only Son, that whoever believes in him shall not perish but have eternal life" (John 3:16). It was to redeem us that Jesus lived and suffered and died. In the agony of Gethsemane and the death at Calvary the infinite love of God met the cost of our redemption. In fact, the infinite price paid by God the Father in sending His Son to die on our behalf should give us an idea of just how valuable we are to Him. Jesus declared, "The Son of Man came to seek and to save the lost" (Luke 19:10). Lost people matter to God. So if I am to be a genuine pastor and disciple of Jesus Christ, then they will matter to me as well. The pastor's role (as well as that of all church leaders) is to instill this value in the heart of the congregation. Therefore, the sacrificial life of Jesus manifests itself on at least two levels. The first is a life of giving—giving of time, resources, and life. The second level is to give our lives in sacrificial giving—even to the point of death.

God is summoning all to live the life that Jesus did. Pastoral ministry or any type of ministry to which God calls members is not about us, but about Him. It is about knowing and serving the Lord.

In Acts 2:44, 45 we read how the early church lived out this truth. "And all those who had believed were together and had all things in common; and they began selling their property and possessions and were sharing them with all, as anyone might have need" (NASB). They understood the great sacrifice that Jesus made for them, and they, in turn, were willing to give sacrificially to others.

One of the things I always did as a pastor was to be the first to go to or for something. I never asked my congregation to do anything that I was not willing to do, or at least something similar to it. When we are the first to begin, whether ministry, evangelism, or giving, we set the model for others to follow. Jesus never asks any of us to do anything that He was not willing to do.

Christ gave His life as a sacrifice for the salvation of the world. The early church gave of their lives and possessions sacrificially out of love for God and people. We are called to do the same. Let us live in the context of eternity, with no attachment to this world. Pastors (and church leaders) who model sacrificial giving will have churches that will do the same.

Paul in 2 Corinthians 5:19 said, "God was in Christ reconciling the world to Himself, not counting their trespasses against them, and He has committed to us the word of reconciliation" (NASB). In other words, God sent His Son to earth to die to save us from our sins and to reestablish our broken relationship with Him, and He has committed this message of salvation and reconciliation to His disciples. The mission of the early church and our mission today are, therefore, the mission of God the Father and the mission of Jesus Christ: to bring back a dying world to the Godhead. But to do that we must ourselves be vitally connected to God as we preach the gospel, meet people's needs, make disciples through the power of the Holy Spirit, and give of ourselves sacrificially to the cause.

Conclusion

While the principles of spiritual leadership that we have looked at apply naturally to the role of the professional minister, they also extend to all people entrusted with spiritual leadership. It may be that another business pays your salary, but if you are involved in the work of the kingdom, the example of Jesus is for you, too. To all those who pastor, coordinate women's ministries, superintend local Sabbath schools, serve as elders, participate in visitation, lead small groups, or otherwise minister, the model of your leadership is found in the Lord Jesus.

As our ideal pastor, He demonstrated to us as spiritual leaders what we should do. First and foremost, we need to deepen our relationship with the Father through prayer and an intimate relationship with Him. Then we will be able to preach the gospel of the kingdom of God and build leaders to take care of the needs of the people. Authentic leadership in the church is about servant leadership. Jesus came to serve, not to be served—to offer His life as a sacrifice. He is calling us to do the same.

---

[1] Recently I went to the library at Andrews University and found more than 40 volumes dealing with the role of the pastor.

[2] Greg Ogden, *Unfinished Business* (Grand Rapids: Zondervan, 2003), pp. 11-15.

[3] Ellen G. White, *Steps to Christ* (Mountain View, Calif.: Pacific Press, 1956), p. 94.

[4] *Ibid.*, p. 70.

[5] A. W. Tozer, *That Incredible Christian* (Harrisburg, Pa.: Christian Publications, 1986), p. 46.

[6] Ellen G. White, *The Desire of Ages* (Mountain View, Calif.: Pacific Press, 1898), p. 171.

[7] Ellen G. White, *The Ministry of Healing* (Mountain View, Calif.: Pacific Press, 1905), p. 143.

[8] E. G. White, *The Desire of Ages,* p. 152.

[9] Philip Samaan, *Christ's Way of Reaching People* (Hagerstown, Md.: Review and Herald Pub. Assn., 1990), pp. 33-40.

[10] E. G. White, *The Desire of Ages*, p. 152.

[11] Robert Coleman, *The Master Plan of Evangelism* (Old Tappan, N.J.: Spire Books, 1963), p. 21.

[12] John W. Frye, *Jesus the Pastor: Leading Others in the Character and Power of Christ* (Grand Rapids: Zondervan, 2000), pp. 115, 116.

Chapter 4

Be a Leader Maker:
Equipping and Motivating the Laity
to Do Great Things for God

How Does the Church Grow?

A growing church is not a one-person show. Church growth is not about what the pastor does—it's about what the members do. Without the members sharing their faith with others and ministering in the world, there is very little chance that the church will thrive and advance. In the research we did on the fastest growing Seventh-day Adventist congregations, it became quite clear to us that such churches spend a great deal of time, resources, and money in training and equipping their members. From interviewing many pastors we discovered that the average one puts in about two hours a week in training members, while the pastors of healthy and growing churches spend 10-15 hours a week in equipping their laity in effective, efficient, and skillful ministry. Moreover, the leaders of the growing SDA churches are also highly intentional in educating others to do their specific ministries. Those congregations have leaders who are focused on training, and members who are eager to learn to do ministry and evangelism. Whether you are a pastor, a leader, or a member, make sure that your church is doing everything it can to create a culture of equipping and training.

Also we found that the average church has either no budget for training or very little. Yet the successful churches spend as much as 10 percent of their budget on it.

The one who leads the way when it comes to training is the pastor or the key leader of the church. Successful pastors spend about one third of their time in preparing members of their congregation for ministry and evangelism. Constantly praying and searching for new leaders, they build a system to foster equipping and training in the church. They strive to make sure that those who work with them are prepared and successful. Because they view people not as competitors but as partners, they continue to shape new leaders and to share ministry. Such pastors understand the value of timing and of being ahead of the curve in change and leadership development.

Thus they follow the instruction of Paul to the young pastor Timothy: "And the things you have heard me say in the presence of many witnesses entrust to reliable people who will also be qualified to teach others" (2 Tim. 2:2). Unfortunately, most churches hire a professional to rob them of their ministry. Most Christians are overfed in knowledge and underexercised in practice. No wonder most congregations are flat or declining. One of the pastors I interviewed said to me, "My church began to grow when I surrendered ministry to my church and my church surrendered leadership to me."

The Biblical Mandate for Training: Focus on Spirituality

Let's begin the concept of training and equipping by looking at the life of Jesus Christ. He is the ultimate leadership builder of the church. If He had not trained His disciples to take on the mantle of leadership, the church would not exist today. His method of discipleship and leadership fostering centered not on what people do, but about what they can become through His transforming power and the presence of the Holy Spirit in their lives. Often in our hurry to get quick results for ministry we concentrate on outcome, technique, and strategy. Jesus always focused on *being* because He knew that if He helped people become what God meant for them to be, they would join Him in His activity in the world. Thus Jesus spent a considerable amount of time discipling His followers in spiritual growth, in character and values, and in loving others as He had loved them.

Christ knew that if He would build a better person, someone filled with the presence of God, grace, wholeness, and attractiveness, He would have an individual willing to be trained and molded to do ministry and evangelism. Such people would want to do ministry because they had experienced the goodness of God. Thus Jesus spent time with His disciples, challenging their spirituality and urging them to connect both with God and with others. A dedicated person serves out of love, a spiritually healthy individual serves with power, and a Spirit-filled Christian serves with effectiveness and grace.

At the heart of our desire for training is our worship of God and our love for others. In fact, that is the heart and essence of church growth. I will never forget what Peter Wagner, one of the foremost authorities in the area of church growth, said in one of his seminars. He declared that we can summarize the essence of church growth by Jesus' saying, "Love the lord your God with all your heart and mind and soul and energy and love your neighbor as you love yourself."

While the world is interested in what people can accomplish and achieve, God is concerned with what people can become. The example of

Jesus in the area of training urges us to do the following: invest our lives in others, build relationships with them, love them, encourage them, and challenge them.

Through instruction, modeling, challenging, and accountability Jesus equipped His disciples for ministry and evangelism. Not only did He teach them about ministry—He showed them how ministry is done, then said, Go and do likewise and come back and report to Me. The core leadership of every church must do a careful analysis of their membership and spot the leaders and potential leaders.[1] The training should include the following: prayer, teaching new ideas and skills, reporting, and accountability (see Mark 6:6-13, 30).

The Most Important Rule in Equipping

When it comes to equipping and training, no one who does ministry should ever do it alone. Yes, it might be a lot more convenient to go to the hospital alone, or teach the best Sabbath school class alone, or present a Bible study alone, but that's not biblical. It's a lot more effective to take someone to the hospital and demonstrate to them how to do ministry. And it's biblical to teach someone how to give Bible studies and lead people to Christ. Jesus even went so far as to say that it's more important to pray for leadership and the harvester than to pray for the harvest.

"Then Jesus went about all the cities and villages, teaching in their synagogues, preaching the gospel of the kingdom, and healing every sickness and every disease among the people. But when He saw the multitudes, He was moved with compassion for them, because they were weary and scattered, like sheep having no shepherd. Then He said to His disciples, 'The harvest truly is plentiful, but the laborers are few. Therefore pray the Lord of the harvest to send out laborers into His harvest'" (Matt. 9:35-38, NKJV).

Every leader should pray that God will raise up still another leader to be trained to do their own ministry. As mentioned earlier, the apostle Paul, commenting on the legacy of modeling, says, "And the things you have heard me say in the presence of many witnesses entrust to reliable people who will also be qualified to teach others" (2 Tim. 2:2).

Notice the chain of progressive events. Every leader must train another leader, who will train another leader, who will train another leader, until Jesus comes. Our Savior prepared the 12 disciples and the 70. The 12 and the 70 mentored the next generation of leaders in the church, and so on.

Ellen G. White on Training

Ellen White saw the value and importance of building new leaders, a concept that she stressed many times. "Ministers should not do the work which belongs to the church, thus wearying themselves, and preventing others from performing their duty. They should teach the members how to labor in the church and in the community."[2]

She went as far as saying that pastors should spend more time training than preaching. That means training is possibly more vital than even preaching and teaching. Of course, she saw the importance of preaching, but it's not enough by itself to fulfill the Great Commission and grow the church. If you want to define the role of the pastor as Ellen G. White saw it, it might well be someone who preaches the gospel and trains others to share their faith with others.

"Every church should be a training school for Christian workers. . . . There should not only be teaching, but actual work under experienced instructors. Let the teachers lead the way in working among the people, and others, uniting with them, will learn from their example. One example is worth more than many precepts."[3]

White also emphasized that the pastors should first train the members to do evangelism so that the whole church can minster together.

"In laboring where there are already some in the faith, the minister should at first seek not so much to convert unbelievers, as to train the church members for acceptable cooperation. Let him labor for them individually, endeavoring to arouse them to seek for a deeper experience themselves, and to work for others. When they are prepared to sustain the minister by their prayers and labors, greater success will attend his efforts."[4]

The research that we did clearly demonstrated this. Without building new leaders, the church might grow on the books but not in attendance. We saw a strong correlation between equipping the members to do evangelism and ministry and bringing the new believers into the church and helping them to grow in the Lord and stay active in the church.

During such training churches should also pay close attention to the spiritual gifts of their members. White admonished all churches to make sure that people are in the proper place in their ministry, as God has made them and wired them. "Let the hand of God work the clay for His own service. He knows just what kind of vessel He wants. To every man He has given his work. God knows what place he is best fitted for. Many are working contrary to the will of God, and they spoil the web."[5]

The Importance of Training in Personal and Church Growth

As I introduce the importance of training in my seminars, I present the audience with the following case study. I start by asking them, If we have a church with 100 people in attendance in a given year and we add 100 more people to that church in that same year, what would be the attendance at the end of that year? Then I continue, Let's take the same church and assume that no one was added to it during that particular year. What would be the attendance at its conclusion? In the case of the first scenario, people tell me that at the end of the year the attendance would be 150, 200, even 250, because some of those who come will bring their families with them, so that the attendance would be higher than 200. In the case of the second scenario, some suggest 100 or 80 people.

Well, what is the correct answer? Based on the research we did on the Adventist Church, people are correct in how they answer the second scenario. The attendance at the end of the year will be about 75-80 people. Why? Because every year someone will die, others will leave the area for whatever reason, and still others will become inactive. Also, since nothing happens during the year, a feeling of pessimism and a negative mood permeates the congregation, which makes it very difficult for it to maintain its current membership. How about the first scenario? Our research shows that the church that adds 100 members to their current attendance of 100 will at the end of the year still have only 100, unless they do the following things:

1. Increase the base of ministry.
2. Increase the base of leadership.
3. Focus on the family.
4. Offer inspiring and dynamic worship.
5. Increase the level of spirituality.
6. Offer a note of hope.

Every church grows in correlation to its effectiveness in meeting the needs of people in discipleship and ministry. It's common sense that if you want to attract people with small kids, you had better have a ministry for kids. And if you want to keep people in the church, have a discipleship ministry.

In the present chapter we will discuss how to increase the base of ministry. Later chapters will deal with many of the other factors listed above.

The Importance and Urgency of Training: A Case Study

Let's imagine that we have a wonderful dynamic woman by the name of Michelle. (I'm choosing a woman here because in our research we discovered that the number of women who do the ministry of nurture is many times higher than that of men.) Michelle loves God, loves people, and loves her church. She has about three or four families that she ministers to. What's important is not whether she does so intentionally or intuitively, but rather the fact that she does it. During the week she will visit the first family when it doesn't come to church, have Bible studies with the second family, and do a lot of social things outside of church time with the third family. In addition, she's discipling the fourth family to do ministry. If any of her families miss church, she calls on them, and if any one of them is in need or trouble, she ministers to them.

Now, let's assume that her congregation is quite active, and throughout the course of the year they add 20 families. The pastor of the church knows that unless someone disciples the new families, they might drift away. He does not have enough leaders and ministers, so he goes to Michelle and tells her, "You are the best when it comes to discipleship— no one does it as well as you do. As you know, the Lord has blessed our congregation this year. He gave us 20 families, but you also realize that unless we disciple them, we're going to lose them." Then he suggests, "How about if you add three or four more families to your load?" Michelle could answer either yes or no. Michelle might say yes, but because of her limited time and resources, she might only end up taking care of a total of four families, because that is her limit. Should she take on more than she can handle, she will become resentful, burdened, overworked, or even angry. What Michelle should have been doing all along was to raise other leaders to do what she is doing. It is also what every one of us should be doing in the church.

Every church grows in proportion to the number of ministries they have. The more it has, the more likely it is to grow. But all ministries depend on a leader that God has inspired. Every minister and leader in the church should pray and seek to duplicate themselves. The base of ministry will never grow unless the base of leadership increases. An important role of leaders is to replicate themselves and make sure that everyone else is successful in what they do.[6] John Maxwell compares those who strive to build others' ministry with those who develop just followers for their ministry.[7]

Leaders Who Develop Followers

- Need to be needed
- Focus on weaknesses
- Hoard power
- Spend time with others
- Grow by addition
- Impact only people they touch personally

Leaders Who Develop Leaders

- Want to be succeeded
- Focus on strengths
- Give power away
- Invest time in others
- Grow by multiplication
- Impact people far beyond their own reach

The Need for Leadership

An old question asks: What came first, the chicken or the egg? But when it comes to ministry and leadership, the answer is settled. There is no doubt about it: the leaders always come first. Without strong and committed leaders there would be no ministry. Churches might do hundreds of ministries but can't because of lack of leadership or resources. God must birth in the heart of a leader a particular kind of ministry or leadership to perform. When God puts it in the heart, He also gives the passion, desire, and skill to do it, and He provides the resources along the way.

Twenty Tips on Equipping the Laity

Whether you are a pastor or a leader in your church, here is a list of some practical ways to train your members for effective ministry and evangelism.

1. Help your congregation to love God and each other. The more people love God, the more they are inclined to do ministry. And the more people love each other, the more they want to serve each other. In essence, make sure people have a heart for God and for others.

2. Give them encouragement. Constantly I run into people who get discouraged because no one affirmed their ministry. Once I met a woman who led a children's division for 20 years. She said to me, "Working with kids can be difficult at time. I wished many times that someone would come to me and thank me for what I am doing or give me some support in any way possible." Making it a habit as a pastor to be the cheerleader of the congregation, I devoted at least two hours every week to telephoning people and encouraging them. And over the course of the years I wrote encouraging notes to everyone in my church. I even bought Taco Bell Dollars and gave them to the teenagers in my church who do some kind of ministry or something nice to someone. (I was very popular with all the teens in my church!)

3. Give them meaningful tasks of eternal significance. Everyone wants to make sure that they will make a difference in the world. Remind them that ministry is about changing lives and helping people and leading them to Jesus.

4. I would make sure that every believer in my team is in the proper position. Do spiritual gifts seminars at least four times a year and follow them up with training seminars on how to do the ministry effectively and with joy and satisfaction. Create a win–win atmosphere. Make sure that they succeed. Nothing can compare to experiencing joy in working side by side with Jesus. If people succeed in what they do, they will be more inclined to do more ministry and evangelism.

5. They must know enough about God and ministry. That is where discipleship and training come in. Many churches just assume that believers will grow and develop the skills themselves. Intentionality is the key.

6. Challenge them to do great things for God. Many people will rise to the occasion if shown the eternal value of what they do. Ministry is not

just about doing something—it is about changing the world and giving people hope and love and eternity.

7. Spot leaders and develop them and deploy them into ministry. I constantly made it a habit as a pastor to look out for the new generation of leaders and to nurture them.

8. Anticipate great things from them. Many churches make the mistake, when they release someone into ministry, of not really expecting much from them, and because of that, they get exactly that. If a church asks individuals to be elders, they respond, "What will it require from me?" The answer often is "Not much," and in return the church receives "not much." People should be told what is required in the context of leading others to salvation, and then be expected to do it. I discovered that if you expect people to accomplish great things, they will—with God on their side—end up doing exactly that.

9. Always bring them into accountability. When Jesus sent His disciples to perform ministry, He asked them to report back to Him (see Mark 6:30). Accountability is essential for growth and encouragement and improvement in spirituality and skills. Meet with your leaders on a frequent basis, especially on Sabbath morning, since that is when they are there and it does not take much time from them.

10. Offer meaningful training programs on a continuous basis. Use Sabbath morning to maximize time. Training should be ongoing and in seminars, as well as on the job. A church should devote 10 percent of its budget to training, bringing guest speakers, buying resource DVDs and books, sending leaders to training events, etc.

11. Build relationships with the members of your congregation. The healthier the relationships, the more inclined they will be to do ministry. Love people and help them to love others. People tend to thrive in an environment of grace and acceptance. Believe that they can fulfill what they seek to do.

12. Show them both the needs and the results. The world is full of hurting and dying people. Our ministry is to restore hope and new life, and to give them a second chance to live. What an awesome ministry to change the world and fill it with grace and love and optimism. Help people see the contribution they are making to eternity and the impact they are having in the world.

13. Personalize the stakes. Ministry is about our children, moms, and dads. It is about the people that we love the most. While it is accurate to say that God died for people in Africa or China, it is infinitely more effective and personal to say that Jesus wants my son and daughter in God's kingdom.

14. Simplify the structure. Make it as easy as possible to do evangelism and ministry. One pastor told me this story. A single mom from his church came to him and asked if she could start a ministry to single mothers. "This is a great idea," he replied. "Let me run it by the individual who is in charge of women's ministries." She agreed that it was wonderful but wanted it approved by her board. They affirmed it and felt the need to give her some budget for babysitting and literature and special programming, a step that had to go to the finance committee. It also felt that it was a winning idea and voted to release the money if the church board OK'd it. The church board approved the request with the support of everyone. But, they said, the church business meeting was just around the corner, so they voted to bring it up at the business meeting so that everyone would know about and support the new ministry. Everyone at the business meeting loved the new ministry and endorsed it enthusiastically. By now, though, one slight problem had surfaced. The woman who had wanted to start the ministry had gotten so frustrated with the whole cumbersome process that she had moved her membership to another congregation and had already started ministering to single moms. It took about eight months from the time of her request to start the ministry until its final approval. Make it as easy as possible for people to start a ministry, and let them know that you are behind them to support them in any possible way.

15. Build structures of equipping. They will lead to a culture of people who prepare others for ministry and simultaneously create more evangelistic fervor in the church.[8] Let everyone train someone else to do their ministry.

16. Teach them that ministry is a God-given gift to every believer, and that it happens everywhere—at home, work, church, etc.

17. Meet with your leaders regularly—visit them in their homes, in their place of business, and in the church, and constantly cast the vision. Equip them through teaching, training, and mentoring. Always own and model ministry, and always remind them that God has called them to change the world and lead people to Him.

18. Pray for new leaders. Claim the promise in Matthew 9:35-37.

19. Model the value of ministry for them. Whatever you ask them to do, you need to be willing to perform also.

20. Honor the church's milestones. Every year, have several Sabbaths during which you recognize God's activity in your church. Acclaim the baptisms, weddings, baby dedications, children's ministry, building projects, debt retirement, and any other good that is happening in your congregation. At the end of the year, have your grand celebration of everything that God has done, and instill the vision of what He will do the following year.

How Do You Motivate People?

What makes people motivated? Four things especially come into play. The first one is fear of loss. People will change if they know that they will lose their job or are threatened by death or illness. Some are influenced by hope of rewards, such as better pay, job, or a life. Yet others are swayed by relationships,[9] such as with people they respect. Finally, the ultimate motivation is our relationship with God and our love for Him. People who love God have traveled everywhere to tell about His love. Those who love God will give of their time, possessions, resources, money, and even their lives for His cause. Therefore, as described earlier in the chapter, the emphasis needs to be on spirituality. Churches will do well to invest in the spiritual development of their members.

Twelve Guidelines for Training Events

Every church must have a system for training and building the new generation of ministers, leaders, and evangelists. Here is a sampling of practices that we saw in some of the healthy churches that we studied.

1. Preach two sermon series on the mission of the church (evangelism, witnessing, ministry, etc.). Preach one series of about six to eight sermons in January and February and another series of three to five sermons (a shorter one) in September. The church needs to be constantly hearing that lost people matter to God and that they must matter to us. The congregational leadership must use every means it has to cast the vision in creative and fresh ways all the time. Creative redundancy is the key. Employ testimonies, small groups, large groups, sermons, slogans, songs, banners, newsletters—whatever means you have. "Vision is usually communicated most effectively when many different vehicles are used: large group meetings, memos, newspapers, posters, informal one-on-one talks. When the same message comes at people from six different directions, it stands a better chance of being heard and remembered, on both intellectual and emotional levels."[10]

2. Devote Sabbath school time for in-depth training to follow up your preaching series: March–April and October–November. We have seen that most people want to be trained, but have no time to do it. Therefore, in order to maximize time, use the Sabbath school for training events.

3. Schedule regular meetings with all the leaders in the church (once a week or month) for encouragement, training, motivation, acquiring new skills, planning new events, etc.

4. Visit every leader in the church and remind them of the spiritually important value of their role. During such occasions, ask people to give three to five hours of their time each week.

5. Visit every ministry in the church. Encourage them and remind them of the eternally important role that they play. Show them that what they do has eternal significance. It is not about performing a job in the church, but about affecting the eternal destiny of others.

6. Disciple at least two leaders every week. Take them out to dinner or visit them in their workplace and remind them that that is their arena of ministry. Pray that God will lead you to these two individuals.

7. Invite guest speakers who have demonstrated the ability to train and motivate and have a proven track record.

8. Turn board meeting sessions into visioning time. Make every board meeting—and for that matter, every committee and ministry meeting—into occasions for worship, prayer, ministry, encouragement, and vision-

A Starting Point

1. Emphasize spirituality, and people will do ministry because of their love and devotion to God.

2. Provide the best worship experience to inspire people to fulfill their calling and potential.

3. Start now. Don't wait. You are already losing time and opportunity.

4. Build upon what you have already done. Add one more person for training every week or month, one more ministry every two or three months.

5. Simplify the structure. Make it as easy as possible for people to do ministry. They cannot thrive in ministry if they must overcome many obstacles and navigate a complicated structure to get going. The role of leadership is to be a cheerleader, helping others to do ministry by removing all obstacles and providing all necessary resources. Unfortunately, many churches put too many roadblocks in front of their members so that they cannot thrive in their purpose of serving God and honoring Him. Effective congregations do everything they can to make it as easy as possible to help their members in fulfilling God's calling. They provide them with opportunities, resources, and training so that they will be successful.

**Start training today, and your church
will have a fantastic tomorrow.**

ing. Then move into the rest of the items as they relate to the mission of the church.

9. Use a variety of ways to convey your mission: preaching, testimonies, slogans, mission statements, meetings, retreats, etc.

10. Send your leaders to training events at least once a year.

11. Allocate 10 percent of your budget for training. Use it to send people for training, for purchasing materials, and for inviting guest speakers.

12. Always emphasize spirituality. Pay very close attention to the spiritual growth of your members and do everything that you can to help them to mature and become fruitful Christians.

How Do You Train Anyone to Do Anything?

The simplest model to train people is to demonstrate on the job. Here is a formula that works effectively.[11] Pour your heart and passion into them. Show them what you are doing and explain to them why. Then turn it over to them as you become a prayer partner and mentor. The best training is always a chain of events that leads to training someone else.

I teach you	you learn
I do	you watch
I do	you help
You do	I help
You do	I watch
You teach	someone else learns

---

[1] See Appendix A, "The Search for Promising Leaders," for helpful suggestions on identifying potential leaders.

[2] *Historical Sketches of the Foreign Missions of the Seventh-day Adventists* (Basel, Switz.: Imprimerie Polyglotte, 1886), p. 291.

[3] E. G. White, *The Ministry of Healing*, p. 149.

[4] Ellen G. White, *Gospel Workers* (Washington, D.C.: Review and Herald, 1915), p. 196.

[5] Ellen G. White, *Lift Him Up* (Hagerstown, Md.: Review and Herald, 1988), p. 65.

[6] Elmer L. Towns and Warren Bird, *Into the Future: Turning Today's Church Trends Into Tomorrow's Opportunities* (Grand Rapids: F. H. Revell, 2000), p. 173.

[7] John Maxwell, *The 21 Irrefutable Laws of Leadership* (Nashville: Thomas Nelson, 1998), p. 210.

[8] Thom S. Rainer, *Effective Evangelistic Churches: Successful Churches Reveal What Works, and What Doesn't* (Nashville: Broadman and Holman, 1996), p. 30.

[9] Leith Anderson, "Volunteer Recruitment," in James D. Berkley, gen. ed., *Leadership Handbook of Management and Administration* (Grand Rapids: Baker Book House, 1994), pp. 280, 281.

[10] John P. Kotter, *Leading Change* (Cambridge, Mass.: Harvard Business School Press, 1996), p. 93.

[11] Many authors have come up with similar models, such as John C. Maxwell, *Contagious Leadership Workshop* (Nashville: Thomas Nelson, 2006), p. 116.

Section 3:

Passionate and Authentic Spirituality

Prioritize Spirituality and Renewal

I am convinced that spirituality and revival should be the main work of the church. The emphasis of the church should be to grow fully devoted disciples of Jesus with a passion to win the world for Him. The most important asset the church has is its members. When they are spiritually healthy, growing, trained, and equipped, they will do great things for God. They will joyfully give of their time and lives for God and His purpose. The book of Acts tells us that because of the love of the New Testament church for Jesus and the urgency of the message, they devoted their time, talents, possessions, and even their lives to the cause of God.

Today people still seek answers in the church for their spiritual needs. But if they do not find them, they will go elsewhere. A Gallup poll reveals that more and more people are obtaining their spiritual experiences outside of the church. James Rutz in *The Open Church,* quoting the Gallup organization, says, "A significant number of 'unchurched' Americans feel there is not enough emphasis on spiritual experiences in the churches." He continues that more of the unchurched than the churched have had a sudden religious experience. They're all charged up, but with no place to go. Gallup noted that a key criticism of the unchurched in regard to religious institutions is that "churches have lost the spiritual part of religion." About one of every five unchurched persons who indicated they had "problems" with churches checked a statement which said, "I wanted deeper spiritual meaning than I found in the church or synagogue."[1] We found that healthy and growing Seventh-day Adventist congregations emphasize spirituality in every aspect of church and Christian life.

Be Intentional About Prayer

Church growth is always closely related to prayer and the power of the Holy Spirit. Before the crucifixion and death of Jesus, the disciples denied Him, abandoned Him, and finally ran away from Him. They were a group of defeated people with no purpose or influence, but when the Holy Spirit came upon them, they turned the world upside down. It was the presence of the Holy Spirit and their connection with Jesus that made the difference, and this came through prayer. Ellen White clearly related renewal to prayer. "A revival need be expected only in answer to prayer."[2]

The Spirit of God brought the world into existence. The Spirit of God brought Jesus Christ back from the dead. The Spirit of God brought the dead bones of ancient Israel to life. And the Spirit of God will bring the dead bones of new Israel back to life. God specializes in doing great and impossible things. The early church did not grow because of programs or talents, but rather because of prayer and the Holy Spirit. Randy Maxwell in *If My People Pray* says, "The church's greatest deficiency today is in power . . . and power for ministry can be released only through prayer."[3]

Thom Rainer in *High Expectation Churches* shows that praying churches tend to grow and keep higher percentages of their members. He writes: "We believe in the programs, plans, emphases, and methodologies we attempt in our church. But ultimately we know that our strength is not from ourselves, but from God Himself. That's why our best assimilation ministry is our prayer ministry. Through fervent prayer we show our dependence upon God."[4]

The present section has three chapters. The first one, "The Jesus-centered Life," deals with both what a disciple of Jesus Christ and an ideal church look like. This chapter is not based so much on the research that we conducted, but on an in-depth Bible study of the book of Acts, especially Acts 2:42-47. I felt that it is vital to give context to the Christian life and to ministry and evangelism. Furthermore, I believe that ministry and witnessing happens in the context of love for God and a sense of pride in the community of faith that we belong to.

The second chapter, "Passion for God's Presence," is a personal testimony about the power of prayer in my own life and ministry. The last church I pastored grew from about 40 people to more than 500 people in attendance. I incorporated this chapter to inspire our congregations to pray more and also to make the point that the greatest need of the church today is not more programs or strategies but the power of God.

The last chapter in this section, "Building a House of Prayer," reflects the research that we conducted about the prayer life of our churches and outlines a strategy to make your church truly become a house of prayer.

---

[1] James H. Rutz, *The Open Church: How to Bring Back the Exciting Life of the First-Century Church* (Auburn, Maine: SeedSowers, 1992), p. 3.

[2] Ellen G. White, *Selected Messages* (Washington, D.C.: Review and Herald, 1958), book 1, p. 121.

[3] Randy Maxwell, *If My People Pray* (Boise, Idaho: Pacific Press, 1995), p. 31.

[4] Thom S. Rainer, *High Expectation Churches* (Nashville: Broadman and Holman, 1999), pp. 174, 175.

Chapter 5

The Jesus-centered Life

The Church We Long For

What is your dream church? That is the question I ask when I do my seminars on church growth or spirituality. People often describe to me a church filled with joy and unity, power and grace, one active and involved in the community, motivated by love for one another and ministry to each other—a church putting God first, praying to Him, studying His Word, worshipping and praising Him. When I hear all of these things, I know that the church they described is also my dream church. It is possible to belong to it. It did exist once and can do so again. What we need is the second coming of the Holy Spirit.

"They devoted themselves to the apostles' teaching and to fellowship, to the breaking of bread and to prayer. Everyone was filled with awe at the many wonders and signs performed by the apostles. All the believers were together and had everything in common. They sold property and possessions to give to anyone who had need. Every day they continued to meet together in the temple courts. They broke bread in their homes and ate together with glad and sincere hearts, praising God and enjoying the favor of all the people. And the Lord added to their number daily those who were being saved" (Acts 2:42-47).

Wouldn't you love to belong to a church like that? Thousands of people all around the world have described for me their dream church, and almost always they sketch one resembling that portrayed in the book of Acts, this picture of vibrant spirituality lived in the context of community. God has created us with the desire to live the wonderful life outlined in His Word, one devoted to His glory and saturated in joy, service, and power.

Acts 2 not only captures our imagination, but speaks intelligently to the issue of practical application. We see illustrated in Acts 2 true Christian commitment: resolution to live wholeheartedly for God and the reorientation of the life to get close to Him by the practice of the spiritual disciplines. The Acts 2 church is the one that God has designed us for, the one that we long for, and the one that we can be part of by God's grace. Taking a closer look at this special church teaches us at least five things about the Christian spiritual life that we'll name first, then picture, and then unpack and explore.

The Jesus–centered Life

Authentic Christian spirituality and church life is

(1) centered on Jesus

(2) empowered by the Holy Spirit

(3) driven by spiritual practices

(4) lived in the context of community

(5) lived in balanced relationships

We can portray this spirituality by using a model that I call the Jesus-centered life.

Life Center Is Jesus Christ

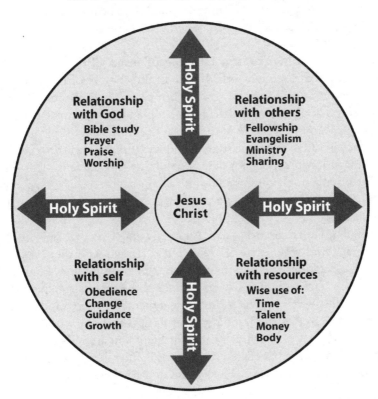

Fragmentation or Integration

Most of us experience fragmented lives. We have our church life and our home life and our devotional life (if we have it at all), but the three remain unconnected to each other, or united with each other in only a weak way. In addition, we have our work and our entertainment, but we are not sure how they can be spiritual in nature. Thus we compartmentalize our lives until they look like a string of unrelated activities: work, home, family, church, devotions, service, recreation, exercise.

But the life that God wants us to live has Jesus as its center, and everything goes back to Him and comes from Him. The organizing principle is Jesus, and the empowering agent is the Holy Spirit. That means that my work, my church life, my devotions, and my family all belong to Him and rest in Him. Those experiencing such a life recognize that it is impossible to live it without the power and grace of the Holy Spirit.

In relation to church growth, imagine what the world would look like if we Christians lived like the early Christians, incorporating Christ's values and vision and life in everything that we did. The home, the marketplace, the church, and the neighborhood would become our place of ministry and evangelism. Because of our love and our lives the world would find itself caught up in the wonder of the Savior.

The Life and Influence of a Disciple of Jesus Christ

How does this model work? In one of the churches I pastored was an engineer who loved God and served Him passionately. James worked for a large corporation with more than 100 people under his direct charge, and he was also extremely active in the life of the church and the community. He preached often, did Bible studies, and went on mission trips. Seeing his love and passionate service for God and the way that the Spirit led and empowered him, people often said to him, "James, you need to be a pastor." His answer was "I am already a pastor who is being paid by the marketplace instead of by the church. No pastor is allowed to be in my engineering firm, but I am there every day. When my employees are hurting, I hurt with them. And when they are rejoicing, I rejoice with them. I pray for them on a rotation basis and invite them over to my home. I am a disciple of Jesus Christ disguised as an engineer," he would conclude. If you looked at the church of which James was a member, you would see 20 engineers who came to the Lord as the result of the ministry of one man.

Imagine what God can do with your life if you are fully committed to Him and have your life centered on Him. Remember that you are a disciple of Jesus Christ disguised as a nurse or a teacher, a physician or even a pastor.

To summarize, the Jesus-centered life model of spirituality is living with passion for the presence of God, experiencing His power and grace continually and rearranging the priorities of life so as to reflect His love, vision, core values, and worldview. Living with a passion for the presence of God changes how we relate to people, to ourselves, and to time, possessions, pleasure, problems, and all of life.

The Jesus-centered Life

The model pictured above visualizes the Jesus-centered life as something like a wheel: Jesus is the center of that wheel, my life is the outer rim, and the Spirit is the spokes. The wheel has four quadrants, each of them representing four areas of relationship: relationship with God, with others, with self, and with resources. My life is centered on Jesus. Everything I do, I do it for His glory with an eye for service, ministry, and evangelism. Christ-centered, Holy Spirit-empowered, and balanced in its relational aspects, such a life is exactly what we see in Acts 2! Let's unpack each of the various elements from the Scriptures.

Centered on Jesus

The early church is a picture of the Lordship of Christ ruling over every area of life—religious, secular, emotional, and physical. It is the integration and balance of the individual and the corporate, the theological and the practical (devotional/ethical), the internal and the external, God and others—but always with Jesus in the center. In Acts 2:36 Peter presents Jesus as Him to whom the people must respond. "Therefore let all the house of Israel know assuredly that God had made this Jesus, whom you crucified, both Lord and Christ" (NKJV). The life we see in Acts 2:42-47 is a response to Christ as Lord, and that makes all the difference.

The church was born out of personal responses to Peter's sermonic appeal to put Jesus as Christ, Savior, and Lord, and out of an empowerment by the Holy Spirit to live holy lives. "Then Peter said to them, 'Repent, and let every one of you be baptized in the name of Jesus Christ for the remission of sins; and you shall receive the gift of the Holy Spirit'" (verse 38, NKJV). Of course, everything in Acts up to this point has laid the foundation for the centrality of Christ and the empowering ministry of the Holy Spirit.[1]

These first believers had an intense passion for God. His kingdom, His purpose, His love, His creation, His people, and His vision for the world dominated their souls. Acts 2 records their desire to learn more about Jesus through study, to be connected to Him through prayer, and to tell the world about Him through evangelism and ministry. "They devoted themselves to the apostles' teaching and to fellowship, to the breaking of bread and to prayer" (Acts 2:42). What comes after chapter 2 tells of their unwavering commitment to live or die for Jesus. Such radical devotion manifested itself not only in their religious observance but also in their use of time and their giving. A life centered on Jesus will be changed in every aspect.

Empowered by the Holy Spirit

The early church was born out of a radical transformation that took place after the Holy Spirit descended upon it. It was when they "were filled with the Holy Spirit" that the otherwise-unremarkable disciples began to preach "as the Spirit enabled them" (Acts 2:4). Furthermore, those that responded to the gospel received "the gift of the Holy Spirit" (verse 38). Any model of Christian spirituality must account for the Spirit of Christ, who, as demonstrated in Acts 2, is the source of direction and power for holy living.[2]

The vibrant church we read about in the book of Acts is a far cry from the ragtag band of disciples that we find in the Gospels. During the last week of the life of Christ it seemed that everything that He did had

Jesus and the Marketplace

As a pastor I was in the habit of visiting my members in the marketplace and reminding them that it was their place of ministry and evangelism and of making a difference for the kingdom of God. On Wednesday afternoon I had a visit with Tammie, a godly and committed Christian physician from our church who owned her own clinic. After lunch I asked her to give me a tour of the place, and when we finished, Tammie and I knelt down and prayed that God would bless her business and turn it into an opportunity for ministry to touch the lives of people for eternity. I said to her, "Tammie, you are a Christian physician. Your work goes beyond physical healing into spiritual transformation. God will send you people that only you can touch and bring to know the love and grace of Jesus." The daughter of a successful public evangelist and pastor, she replied, "I never thought about it this way." Whatever your profession, your home and business are your primary places of ministry. Turn them into opportunities to make a difference for the kingdom of God.

failed—and failed miserably. By Thursday and Friday of that week one of the disciples had denied Jesus, others had abandoned Him, and some had even run away from Him (Mark 14:50-52; Luke 22:54-60). But this same group of people later turned the world upside down by their witness and boldness. The shift in the disciples did not result from some seminar they took in leadership or evangelism, or from some sort of self-improvement course, but was a result of the presence of the transformational power of the Holy Spirit. "But you will receive power when the Holy Spirit comes on you" (Acts 1:8).

Ellen G. White explains the incredible change that the Holy Spirit produces in the individual. "The Christian's life is not a modification or improvement of the old, but a transformation of nature. There is a death to self and sin, and a new life altogether. This change can be brought about only by the effectual working of the Holy Spirit."[3] The Scriptures testify, too, that "if anyone is in Christ, the new creation has come: The old has gone, the new is here! All this is from God" (2 Cor. 5:17, 18).

The Holy Spirit gave the church the power to live in the kingdom of God while they were still here on earth. They had a taste of eternity in their hearts. In the same manner, God's grace will move upon us as it did on the early church and enable us to live the life of Jesus with effectiveness. The greatest need of the church today is not more programs or techniques or books or seminars—it is to be filled, guided, moved, and controlled by the Holy Spirit.

The Adventist Church stands at a crossroads. We have lost the passion that our pioneers had, and are not sure how to capture it again. Some voices direct us to go back to the past and live as our founders did. Others say, "No, all that we need is to be relevant and loving." I believe that what we really must do is to recapture the experience of the early church by being filled with the power and effectiveness of the Holy Spirit—driven by passion for the lost, compelled with the urgency of the Second Coming.

Driven by Spiritual Practices

Christian disciplines are spiritual practices that facilitate growth in our relationship with God. The list recorded in the book of Acts includes Bible study, prayer, ministry, evangelism, fellowship, giving and sharing, worship, praise, joy, and simplicity. The earliest Christians found that such spiritual exercises enabled them to advance in the Christian experience both individually and corporately.[4] Though this passage does not record all of them, it has a higher concentration of spiritual disciplines than any other place in the Bible. Because of limitations of space, we will highlight only a few of the most prominent.

It was a learning church. "They devoted themselves to the apostles' teaching" (Acts 2:42). Constantly they listened to the apostles teach the Word of God.[5] Believers had an intense passion to learn everything they could about God and His ways. One of the most compelling challenges the church faces today is lack of biblical understanding and application. Because the riches of Christ are inexhaustible, authentic spirituality integrates continuous learning into the Christian experience. We may ever be discovering more and more about Him (Eph. 1:17-19) and daily advancing in Christian knowledge and growth (2 Cor. 3:17, 18). In the area of church growth it became clear to us that the more we know about Jesus, the more we want to share Him with others.

Though some people believe the myth that growing churches ignore or marginalize the Bible, they do, in fact, teach the Bible, but they explain it in understandable language. Their teaching ministries are relevant, interesting, and practical. One pastor in our research study said, "I teach in order to touch the heart." Another pastor commented, "When I stand in the pulpit, I am not thinking about exegetical scholars. I am thinking about the gas station attendant and the bank teller: what do they need to hear from God and how can I share His message with them?"

It was a praying church. The book of Acts contains numerous references to prayer. In fact, we might as well call it the book of prayer. Early believers prayed when things were going well and when the situations looked grim (Acts 4:23-31; 12:5, 12). They prayed when they had crises and when they had praises. Living lives of connectedness with God, they truly believed that the power is in God and the way to release it is through prayer. "They devoted themselves . . . to prayer" (Acts 2:42).

Prayer was essential to the life of the community. They depended upon God and sought His direction and power and actively submitted themselves to His will and purpose.[6] And Jesus makes it clear that without a connection to Him, we can do nothing. He said, "Remain in me, as I also remain in you. No branch can bear fruit by itself; it must remain in the vine. Neither can you bear fruit unless you remain in me. I am the vine; you are the branches. If you remain in me and I in you, you will bear much fruit; apart from me you can do nothing" (John 15:4, 5). But with Him we can do great things for the kingdom of God. Prayer, such as that to which the early believers devoted themselves, connects the soul to God and has a vivifying influence.

As we studied successful Adventist churches, we discovered that they displayed a strong emphasis on prayer, manifested in praying pastors and leaders and average members, too. Committee meetings prioritized prayer, and the congregations provided opportunity for prayer before, during, and after the weekly worship service. In addition, successful churches established prayer partnerships. In other words, prayer pervaded the place.

I have been encouraging Christians to pray regularly for five individuals and to minister to and love them. As a result I have seen many people come to the Lord because of prayer. Why don't you join me in praying for five people and let us see what God can do!

It was a fellowshipping church. "They devoted themselves . . . to fellowship" (Acts 2:42). Believers met to worship and associate every day of the week. Filled with togetherness and love, it was a dream church of community, healing, and love. Their fellowship was an outgrowth of their attachment to Christ. The early believers had common hope, faith, love, struggles, goals, and destiny, and that brought them into intimate relationship.

Biblical fellowship is always born of and nurtured by mutual fellowship with God. I have discovered that my bonds to some people are based on mutual interest, while those with my brothers and sisters in the Lord are based on our love and commitment to Jesus. Authentic brotherhood and fellowship are found in Christ (Eph. 2:14; Gal. 3:26–28). Fellowship with people who seek to grow into Christlikeness is irresistible and meaningful. When this takes place, we discover that our health and growth are linked to our involvement with the community.[7]

Going to church is not identical to having biblical fellowship. Our fellowship with others is grounded in our fellowship with God. "We proclaim to you what we have seen and heard, so that you also may have fellowship with us. And our fellowship is with the Father and with his Son, Jesus Christ. We write this to make our joy complete" (1 John 1:3, 4). Jesus is the heart and breath and foundation of Christian community. No true fellowship can possibly exist without Christ's Spirit in us and between us. Jesus is what we have in common.[8]

Growing churches of today, like the model church in Acts 2, place a strong emphasis on fellowship. One vibrant Adventist church feeds its members twice every Sabbath: breakfast and lunch. A wonderful atmosphere and spirit exists as these Christians break bread together and associate over food. How can your church encourage regular spiritual fellowship between its members?

It was a sharing church. "All the believers were together and had everything in common. They sold property and possessions to give to anyone who had need" (Acts 2:44, 45). From their sacred fellowship flowed a supernatural generosity. Not considering their resources as their own, they loved each other to the point of selling their possessions for the good of the community.[9]

True fellowship is more than what we share in together—it is also what we share out together. All the things that the first Christians owned in life belonged to Jesus, and they used them to His glory and honor. They gave not grudgingly or reluctantly but generously and in joy and love for the advancement of the cause of the kingdom of God and the betterment of other people and the world.

Spirituality is being like Christ, which means living in self-giving love. A real Christian cannot bear to have too much when others have too little. When the world sees our love and care, they will be much more inclined to join us and accept Jesus as Lord and Savior.

Growing churches are intentional about meeting the needs of those in their own congregations, rallying around the sick and the hurting, the needy and the weak. People pray for one another, share their financial resources with each other, and enjoy strong hospital visitation programs. This is the Acts 2 way.

Our research revealed that growing congregations are also heavily involved in the life of their communities. We have seen the emergence of new approaches. Instead of depending on a Dorcas outpost, many churches are offering innovative services to their communities, such as financial planning seminars, classes for potty training toddlers, courses in English as a second language, and weight-loss support groups.

It was a worshipping church. To worship God is to honor Him and reverence Him as divine. It is to adore, respect, and esteem God as the source of life and the ruler of the universe (Rev. 4:8-11). In other words, to worship is to act as an inferior before a superior. When I worship God, I am saying by my actions, "God, You are better than I am. You are bigger than I am. You are more than I am." That was the experience of the early church.

The worship of the Acts 2 community manifested itself in praise and thanksgiving (Acts 2:47). Worship also led them to meet together daily with joy. They were able to say as did David, we "rejoiced with those who said to [us], 'Let us go to the house of the Lord'" (Ps. 122:1). Such worship motivated them to give generously of their time, talents, position, and even their lives. Thus they experienced what true worship is all about—having God sit on His throne in the center of the universe and also the throne that stands in the center of the heart.

Praise had been an outward sign of the indwelling of the Spirit. When the Holy Spirit fills us with the things of God, we will manifest a spirit of worship and praise and a life permeated with joy. The musical expression of that praise need not fit into a single category. Some growing Adventist churches have traditional services, others use contemporary music, but most of them enjoy a blend of the traditional and contemporary. The important idea is that it is the presence of God, not the activities of the worshippers, that draw people into the authentic worship of growing churches. When women and men experience the joy of God's companionship in the worship service, they will return and bring a friend.

Lived in the Context of Community

As part of the early church's balanced portrait of spirituality we find in Acts 2 a powerful description of the connection between the individual believer's experience and the corporate Christian life. In this wholistic model we see that the believers had a powerful connection with God and also a strong and intentional bond with fellow believers and with their community, neighbors, and associates. Their lives were so desirable that they held the favor of all the people and "the Lord added to their number daily those who were being saved" (Acts 2:47).

If our spirituality is focused only on a relationship with God, we become monks. Yet if our attention is only on our human relationships, we become social workers. True and authentic spirituality nurtures a vertical relationship with God and horizontal relationships with others. Jesus admonishes us, "'Love the Lord your God with all your heart and with all your soul and with all your mind and with all your strength.' The second is this: 'Love your neighbor as yourself.' There is no commandment greater than these" (Mark 12:30, 31).

Any credible model of spirituality must include the development of the personal spiritual life in the context of community. Spiritual growth and our desire to become like Jesus cannot be reliably sustained outside of a like-minded fellowship. While we need to do many things in order to grow spiritually, our effort is incomplete unless we also intentionally seek to live among and contribute to the lives of others. What we read in Acts 2 is that this community consisted of people who had made an individual decision for Christ and who also fully participated in life together: studying, praying, sharing, worshipping. Jesus started the pattern, and it is what the church continued to do.

It was to the name of Christ that the first disciples responded (Acts 2:36-38), but it was to the number of the church that they were added (verse 47), and within that body they demonstrated a love for all both within and outside the bounds of their fellowship. Their example of spirituality stresses that a strong relationship with God will always motivate us to live for His glory, and living for His glory means embracing others with His love. The closer we are drawn to Jesus, the more fully we will love others (Col. 3:12-15).

Lived in Balanced Relationships

The Acts 2 spirituality of the early church nurtured four major relationships: with God, with others, with self, and with resources and time in the context of God and His will.

A relationship with God. Not only did the first converts worship and praise God, pray and study the Bible, but they did all of that with the utmost devotion and commitment. God was the center of their lives, and they did everything to demonstrate that He was. Prayer, study, worship, and meditation are spiritual exercises that encourage a healthy relationship with Him.

Relationships with others. When the flame of the Spirit descended upon the gathered disciples, it turned their attention outward to the crowd. And when 3,000 became part of their number that day, the believers continued to foster fellowship as a spiritual practice. The book of Acts lists it along with prayer and devotion to apostolic teaching. We manifest our relationships with others through our commitment to love and honor them, to hear them and serve them. Some activities helpful for developing health in this area of spirituality are those of fellowship, evangelism, ministry, encouragement, and love.

A relationship with self. Starting with the initial repentance and including everything that came afterward, the character of the early church was predicated on the grace of God and individual choice. In biblical spirituality, personal choice plays a crucial role. Just as the early converts responded to Peter's call and then chose to devote themselves to the Christian way, so also is our spirituality partially dependent upon our choice. Our relationships with God and others stem from our relationship with ourselves, a commitment that we make to live totally and wholeheartedly for the glory of God. It is also about allowing God to change us into His image (2 Cor. 3:17, 18; Rom. 12:1, 2). Some of the ways that this relationship reveals itself in our lives include obedience, the changing of heart and mind, and personal growth.

A relationship with resources. A fundamental component in spirituality is a dedication of the entire life to God. "Therefore, I urge you, brothers and sisters, in view of God's mercy, to offer your bodies as a living sacrifice, holy and pleasing to God—this is your true and proper worship. Do not conform to the pattern of this world, but be transformed by the renewing of your mind" (Rom. 12:1, 2). From this flows a change in how we relate to what we used to call our own: time, talents, money, possessions, and bodies. The wise use of resources, regular giving, and healthful living are demonstrations of a healthy attitude toward resources. As an outgrowth of their relationships with God, others, and themselves, the early Christians had a radical relationship to resources, sharing everything that they owned and spending all for the kingdom. They gave because they loved God, and they gave radically because they loved radically (2 Cor. 8:1-15).

Conclusion

Spirituality is about the whole of life and the entire person. The picture of the church that we have in the book of Acts speaks to a wholistic spirituality addressing the totality of the experience of the believer. Just as sinfulness touches every aspect of our person, so does positive spiritual living. Spirituality is never about going to church once or twice a week or reading the Bible occasionally or praying from time to time. It permeates everything that we do and say and think. It is what defines us and sets us apart.

The life we dream about, the life that God dreams about for us and His church, the life described in Acts 2, is one centered on Jesus, empowered by the Holy Spirit, driven by spiritual practices, lived in the context of community, and guided by balanced relationships. And everyone loved the Acts 2 church. They were "praising God and having favor with all the people. And the Lord added to the church daily those who were being saved" (Acts 2:47, NKJV).

One of the questions we asked people in our research was "If your church were removed from this community, would it miss you?" We got many different answers, but the most common one was "I do not think they even know we are here." My prayer is that your church will serve its community in such powerful and effective ways that if we take it away, the people of your community will have hard time functioning without your love, service, and care.

---

[1] The book opens with the ascension of Jesus and a note that even up to that point He had given "instructions through the Holy Spirit" (Acts 1:2). It then follows with Christ's promise of the baptism of the Holy Spirit that will empower their witness to Him (verses 5, 8). This passage closes with the promise of Christ's return (verse 11). The second chapter records the testimony about Jesus empowered by the Holy Spirit (Acts 2:1-36), which then leads to a call to respond to Jesus Christ and receive the Holy Spirit.

[2] G. Edwin Bontrager and Nathan Showalter, *It Can Happen Today!* (Scottsdale, Pa.: Herald Press, 1986), pp. 20, 21.

[3] E. G. White, *The Desire of Ages*, p. 172.

[4] Adele Ahlberg Calhoun, *Spiritual Disciplines Handbook: Practices That Transform Us* (Downers Grove, Ill.: IVP Books, 2005), pp. 36-40.

[5] Dennis Gaertner, *Acts: The College Press NIV Commentary* (Joplin, Mo.: College Press, 1993), pp. 82, 83.

[6] Darrell L. Bock, *Acts, Baker Exegetical Commentary on the New Testament* (Grand Rapids: Baker Pub. Group, 2007), p. 151.

[7] C. H. Dodd, in George Panikulam, *Koinonia in the New Testament* (Rome: Biblical Institute Press, 1979), p. 3.

[8] Lloyd J. Ogilvie, *Acts, The Communicator's Commentary* (Waco, Tex.: Word, 1983), pp, 74, 75.

[9] C. K. Barrett, *Acts: A Shorter Commentary* (London: T. & T. Clark, 2002), p. 33.

Chapter 6

Passion for God's Presence

I was an enthusiastic young pastor attending my first denominational ministerial meetings. A conference official stood in front of 100 pastors, and, raising a set of papers, announced, "Now we have a program that will finish the work." Wanting to go home to heaven, I got excited. Well, as you realize, the work did not get finished, and we are still here.

Two years later the same individual stood in the same spot and proclaimed, "Now we have a program that will finish the work." Again I became excited. But sadly, we're still here. After another two years someone else declared to the assembled ministers, "*Now* we have a program that will finish the work!" This time I paid no attention, realizing that none of those programs were going to do anything.

Evangelistic programs and church growth techniques are great and wonderful (and apparently reproducing like rabbits). The only problem is that they don't work without power.

Even a Mercedes-Benz—one of the best-engineered automobiles in the world—will not move without fuel. And what we need is not a better-engineered strategy but a source of power.

We all know that there is something wrong with the church of today. We dream of a vibrant Christ-worshipping community of faith that evangelizes the world with love and power, a church triumphant with the Spirit. What we see instead are congregations in plateau or decline, composed of people who are enthusiastic about worldliness and apathetic about their faith. Something's wrong here.

One author lists the top 10 problems facing the church as apathy, shallowness, worldliness, failure to give, pastoral burnout, teenage dropout, fear of evangelism, flabby self-discipline, maxed-out schedules (with no real results), and a chronic shortage of strong and committed individuals. It is what he calls "The State of the Church Today."[1]

But what was the state of the New Testament church? It was sold-out discipleship turning the world upside down with its message and life. Spreading like wildfire across cultures, hurdling the obstacles of paganism, persecution, and Pharasaism, it turned the world upside down. It was powerful!

Many years ago A.W. Tozer wrote, "If the Holy Spirit was withdrawn from the church today, 95 percent of what we do would go on and no one would know the difference. If the Holy Spirit had been withdrawn from the New Testament church, 95 percent of what they did would stop, and everybody would know the difference."[2] Today, more than anything else, we need that Holy Spirit!

Not by Might

When we depend too much on human effort, we rely too little on divine power. We think that if we had a youth pastor or a better preacher or a better choir or better school or better building, then the church would succeed. Such things are good, but they're not the panacea for our ill congregations. After we've attended every seminar, tried every strategy, checked off every task, we'll find ourselves in the same spot—only more tired.

The Scriptures give us a holy prescription. "This is the world of the Lord to Zerubbabel: 'Not by might nor by power, but by my Spirit,' says the Lord Almighty" (Zech. 4:6). The word "might" means every conceivable human ingenuity. We think that the work of God will get done by what we do, through the programs that we develop, the resources we have, and the talents we exhibit. Yet God reminds us that none of them accomplish things of eternal significance. What really works—in converting people, in growing the kingdom, in living in God's friendship—is the Spirit of the Lord.

Another book. Another plan. Another seminar. Another "Five Steps to Transforming Something or Other." They are not the answer. We don't need more formulas—we need more *filling*. We don't need more plans—we need more *power*. And we don't need more strategies—we need more *Spirit*.

Ministry Unplugged

At the heart of our problem is a disconnect—we are missing the vital connection to the Vine. Without Jesus there's no life. He tells us, "Remain in me, as I also remain in you. No branch can bear fruit by itself; it must remain in the vine. Neither can you bear fruit unless you remain in me. I am the vine; you are the branches. If you remain in me and I in you, you will bear much fruit; apart from me you can do nothing" (John 15:4, 5).

One of the churches that I pastored had, at one time, 80 members, but they had a great vision. They met together one day and decided that they would like to have a structure that would seat 600 people. During the next few years the congregation grew to about 100 in attendance, and it started to prepare for their dream church. But in the process of designing the new building they began fighting, and the attendance dropped to about 40 and stayed there for one year.

That's when I arrived to be their pastor. I accepted the invitation to this church because I wanted to be a church growth expert. At that time I was working on my doctoral degree in leadership and church development. I used all the things I had learned, implementing the strategies, plans, and programs from my classes and seminars. For three and a half years I employed every technique I knew, working 60 to 80 hours every week. My wife joined me 30 to 40 hours every week, too. Then something unusual happened.

After three and a half years of intense effort and cutting-edge methods, attendance went from 40 to 30. I had become a church decline expert.

I spent those three and a half years doing ministry unplugged from the source of life, separated from the Vine. I had forgotten the most important ingredient in healthy church development: the power of God. God is the one who grows His church. Our role is total and radical reliance on Him.

"The first lesson to be taught the workers in our institutions is the lesson of dependence upon God. Before they can attain success in any line, they must, each for himself, accept the truth contained in the words of Christ: 'Without me ye can do nothing.'"[3] What Ellen White calls the first lesson I had learned as the last lesson. It is easier for me to implement plans or strategies than to surrender my heart, plans, and ideas to His will.

The Fantastic Future

What is God's solution for us? What does He want? How can we recapture the vitality of the early church? Christ declared to His followers just before He went into heaven: "But you will receive power when the Holy Spirit comes on you; and you will be my witnesses in Jerusalem, and in all Judea and Samaria, and to the ends of the earth" (Acts 1:8).

Here's what happened: They waited on the Lord. They prayed. They received power when the Holy Spirit filled them. And then—and only then—did they go out evangelizing the world with the gospel.

Whether or not the disappointed little group of disciples believed the promise of Jesus, they did the right thing. They trudged back down the hill into the city and "with one accord devoted themselves to prayer, together with the women and Mary the mother of Jesus, and with his brothers" (verse 14, RSV).

They gave themselves to prayer. But didn't serious men and women have more important things to engage their attention? After all, German barbarians were again raiding across the Rhine, conspirators sought the life of Emperor Tiberius in Rome, and famine had spread through the Roman Empire. Most people still think that those are the kinds of issues that really matter. And they do matter. But all the disciples did was to go home and pray—and that's really the important thing, because prayer can do what no power on earth can.

We must understand our need for prayer. If biblical exhortations aren't clear enough, let us look to our own years of frustrated ministry as evidence that we can no longer continue relying on human effort and doing church unplugged from the Power source. Our only option is to commit ourselves to God's solution: prayer. The commitment to God's solution is what gave Gideon a miraculous victory over a foreign army. Through the power of God 300 people defeated a vastly larger military force. They achieved victory not by means of their strength but by means of God's strength. This is what we need today. An army marches on its feet, but the church of God marches on its knees. That is the power of God—the power we need today.

The church has a fantastic future, because all things are possible with God. "The Lord is willing to do great things for us. We shall not gain the victory through numbers, but through the full surrender of the soul to Jesus. We are to go forward in His strength, trusting in the mighty God of Israel."[4] Prayer is the way forward to revival, power, and growth.

The Means of Renewal

"If my people, who are called by my name, will humble themselves and pray and seek my face and turn from their wicked ways, then will I hear from heaven, and I will forgive their sin and will heal their land" (2 Chron. 7:14). Here is the essence of renewal—the promise of God for us today.

It would be well for us to consider the five conditions for renewal embedded in this text. 1. We belong to God and are His people. 2. We must call on His name. 3. We must humble ourselves, which means removing egotism and self-interest from our lives. 4. We must pray, seeking Him. 5. We must repent of our sins. Then God will hear our cries and will answer our prayers and will renew us. It is not some program that we buy into, but an organic relationship with God. Instead of a strategy, it is a commitment to the Lord Jesus Christ.

Ellen White wrote about our part in renewal: "A revival of true godliness among us is the greatest and most urgent of all our needs. To seek this should be our first work. . . . But it is our work, by confession, humiliation, repentance, and earnest prayer, to fulfill the conditions upon which God has promised to grant us His blessing. A revival need be expected only in answer to prayer."[5] Renewal occurs when people take God very seriously and spend considerable time seeking Him. "We may be assured of this: the secret of all failure is our failure in secret prayer."[6]

After my church declined from 40 to 30 attendees, I decided to quit the ministry and go back to engineering. *I will make more money and will have my weekends off, and I won't have to deal with difficult people*, I thought. I typed my letter of resignation on my computer, and as I finished, the doorbell rang. When I went to the door, my wife happened across the letter and later asked me why I wanted to leave pastoral ministry.

"It's very simple," I explained. "I have calculated that if the current trend continues, in three and a half years there will be only you and I left in the church. I don't want that to happen. I want an honorable exit—as honorable as it can be." My wife looked at me and said simply, "Have you been praying for your church?" I thought that was a bit judgmental and harsh. I started to defend myself, but pretty soon I had lost the argument, because deep inside I had to admit that I was more into strategic planning and programming than into prayer and spirituality.

With the encouragement of my wife, I decided to spend one day a week in prayer and fasting. I was supposed to eat my last meal on Sunday night and go to the church to spend all of Monday in prayer. That first Monday morning my wife said to me as I was leaving, "Pray as if your life depends on it." I told her that I didn't know what that meant, but that I would do my best. Entering the church, I knelt down in front of one of the pews to pray for the family that sat on it. After two minutes of prayer, I found myself sound asleep, and I slept eight hours that day. Ordinarily I never sleep during the day, but my attempt at prayer seemed to change all that.

My biggest challenge that day was knowing what to tell my wife when I got home. She asked how it went, and I mumbled something about "great," and in my heart I added, "for the two minutes that it lasted." But with her encouragement I kept at it. The next week I spent three minutes in prayer, and the next week four, then down to three and up to five. It was then that I made the most important spiritual discovery of my life: I was the greatest challenge to my spirituality. Not the distraction of the Internet or the radio or the TV or sports. I found that I wasn't wired to do this. Give me a program or a strategy or something to do, and I would do it. Spirituality is about two things that are completely contrary to our culture and values and worldviews and nature. It involves a submissive life and a connectedness with God.

My wife continued with her encouragement and I in my commitment. "I will do it and keep doing it, even if it kills me," I told myself. Luckily, it didn't kill me. As time passed, things in my life started to change. An amazing thing happened.

For eight months I continued this prayer effort, and the first few weeks of determination and struggle eventually turned into joy and peace. In my newfound enthusiasm, I started to look for additional ways to incorporate prayer in my life, and practiced one hour of prayer as I walked every day. I began to be filled with hope and optimism. My preaching and ministry became more effective. The discipline of prayer was changing me.

Then one Sabbath as I preached from the pulpit I saw the same faithful 30—plus four more: a husband, wife, and two little daughters. *They must be from out of town,* I thought to myself. I didn't consider that they might be seekers—at that time our church was so depressing, I wouldn't have attended it myself except for the fact that I was the pastor.

Greeting them at the door, I asked if they were visiting in the area. He said that they lived across the street. Now I was dying to know why they were there! "I fished up in Alaska, and my boss up there used to be an Adventist," he told me. "Every evening he'd gather the crew and talk about his philosophy of life. In one of those sessions he told us, 'If you ever go to church, it has to be the Seventh-day Adventist Church—they have the truth.'"

When this man returned home, he forgot what his employer had said about church, and life went on as before. But one day his wife said to him, "Look, we have two daughters, and we need to take them to church. I used to go to the Catholic Church. Let's go back."

"Absolutely not," the husband replied. "My boss said it has to be the Adventist Church or no church." She said she didn't care which one it was, as long as it was a church. So there they were on Sabbath morning in my congregation.

They were hungry for God. I studied the Bible with them twice a week, and two months later baptized them. When I baptized them, I dedicated the sermon to them, and as I shared their story, I shared my own story too. I told my congregation about my struggle with prayer, and how I used to come into the church and pray for them. I told them how I had prayed that God would send me someone to baptize. "The God of the whole universe was listening to the prayers of a discouraged pastor in the middle of nowhere in the state of Washington, and He gave me this couple."

As soon as I said this, a 69-year-old man stood up, came to the front, and started to cry. "I have four grown children," he told the whole congregation, "and all of them are far from the Lord, but if God answered the prayers of Pastor Joe and gave him this family, I know that He will answer my prayer and give me my children and their families. I'm going to pray for them, day and night. I want you to pray for them and for me. Hold me accountable. Remind me that God answers prayer." As soon as he finished, a woman from the other side of the room shared a similar conviction.

During that one Sabbath morning more than 10 people gave similar testimonies. It started a movement of prayer that spread like a wildfire. People started to pray before, during, and after church, during the week, and on the weekends. They prayed individually and in groups, but always with passion. Eight years later that church had grown from 30 defeated people to about 500 fully devoted followers of Jesus. Those 30 people without purpose became 500 people who turned their city upside down. And they went from 30 people who came to church out of obligation to 500 who met to worship God and give Him glory.

God did an awesome thing. All the church growth strategies that I implemented did not work. But prayer transformed my life and that of the congregation. Prayer changed my life, and I know it will change yours. Just as prayer altered my church, so it will yours.

When we tried every technique, we failed. But when we tried God, we succeeded. God is faithful to His promises. He will do great things for us if we surrender ourselves to Him. And He wants to repeat this success story again and again and again—starting with you.

We're busy people. Deadlines loom ahead of us, appointments press in around us, tasks demand our attention every hour. In all this busyness we tend to ignore the one true priority. Let us reject busyness and answer the whispered invitation of God to commune with Him.

Means of Power

One afternoon I spent two hours sawing at a tree in my backyard. It and another one beside it were growing too close to the house and were endangering it. So taking my hand saw and my masculinity, I marched outside to cut it down. Two hours of hard work with my saw, and I had managed to make a big scrape in the side of the tree. Every day I spent an hour or two sawing at this tree, and after two weeks it finally came down. My neighbor, moved to pity—by my grunting and groaning, perhaps—brought his chain saw over. He brought down that second tree, doing in a few minutes what it had taken me weeks to accomplish.

That's something like the difference between God's power and ours. The tragedy of too many Christian lives is the substitution of human effort in the place of divine strength. The results have been too obvious. When we try to accomplish by human means what can be done only by spiritual ones, we embezzle God's authority.

The words "power" and "prayer" appear numerous times throughout the book of Acts. Prayer is the means by which God releases His power into our world.

The problem the church struggles with is not a lack of power. Infinite power is available for the asking. No, the difficulty is rather with us. We don't call for the power, and then we complain that we don't have it. In many ways we are more naive than even the Arab chieftains that Lawrence of Arabia brought with him to the Paris Peace Conference after World War I. These men of the desert were amazed at many things, but nothing astonished them half as much as the running water in their hotel bathroom. In the desert, water was a scarce resource, but here they could have it simply by the turning of a tap, free and seemingly exhaustless.

As they were preparing to leave Paris, Lawrence found them trying to detach the faucets so that out in the dry desert they might have water. He tried to explain that behind the flowing taps were huge reservoirs of water and that without such a supply the faucets were useless. But the Arabs were sure that these magic instruments would give them water forever.

Are we not even more credulous in our Christian living? In the Holy Spirit are deep reservoirs of power, wells of water springing up into everlasting life. But the Holy Spirit cannot flow through a closed tap—He cannot work through an unyielding life.[7]

So open the taps—taps really connected to an infinite source. The promise of power is for any who will believe and receive. And when by faith and grace we turn the taps and the power flows, watch out! "And with great power the apostles gave witness to the resurrection of the Lord Jesus Christ. And great grace was upon them all" (Acts 4:33, NKJV).

Abraham prayed—just one man—and Lot was delivered from the fiery destruction of Sodom and Gomorrah. Moses prayed—just one man—and the waters of the sea parted. Joshua prayed—just one man—and the walls of Jericho crashed down. David prayed—just one man—and the stone from his slingshot was guided to the forehead of Goliath, and the giant fell dead. Elijah prayed—just one man—and fire poured down from heaven and consumed the sacrifice. Daniel prayed—just one man—and the mouths of lions were closed. Esther prayed—just one woman—and God delivered the whole nation of Israel from complete destruction

If you listen you might hear people in your church holding on to the *If* faucet. If we had a better pastor. If we had a better program. If we had better people. If we had more resources. If we had something else, we would be able to do spectacular things. Evangelism and church growth would overflow our pews and fill up our church budget buckets. But it is not by might or by power, but by the Holy Spirit that God's work will be done. If the faucet is not connected to a reservoir of water, it will only disappoint.

Jesus is still praying for His disciples: "You shall receive power when the Holy Spirit has come upon you; and you shall be witnesses to Me" (Acts 1:8, NKJV), witnesses to a dry and thirsty world. You shall be My witnesses that the Savior has come, that He will return again, and that His Spirit is already here.

Means of Growth

The size of the church on the morning of Pentecost Sunday was 120. By the evening it had 3,120 people worshipping God together in the name of Jesus Christ. Then God added 5,000 more, growing it to 8,120. After that, the book of Acts does not give us a specific membership number, but just declares that the church was multiplied (see Acts 6:1, 7). This baby church with its phenomenal growth did not expand because of its programs, techniques, or strategies. The secret behind its expansion was God: His power, His Spirit, His effectiveness. If the church today is going to experience the same thing, it must return to its original pattern and be controlled by the Holy Spirit.

I was in Milan, Italy—one of the most secular cities in the world—a few years ago to give a vision for prayer and a challenge to prayer. One of the churches of Milan, in the heart of Italy's industrial and financial and fashion center, caught the vision. Its members started to pray and turned their church into a house of prayer. They prayed for their church, community, and friends and relatives. In about a year God had grown that church from 35 people to 180. If God can do it in Milan, couldn't He do it in your city?

"The reason why our preachers accomplish so little is that they do not walk with God. He is a day's journey from most of them."[8] Ellen White there tells us that our ineffectiveness results not from theological error or ignoring the latest strategies but from of our lack of connection with God. Oswald Chambers put it well: "The lasting value of our public service for God is measured by the depth of the intimacy of our private times of fellowship and oneness with Him."[9]

God is calling us to be with Him. Only then can He send us out to preach, teach, love, and change the world. This happens through the power of the Holy Spirit. Jesus "appointed twelve, so that they would be with Him and that He could send them out to preach, and to have authority to cast out the demons" (Mark 3:14, 15, NASB).

And Jesus has called *you* to be with Him. Enter into the presence of God. Worship and love Him. Give yourself as a living sacrifice to Him. "Those who do not learn every day in the school of Christ, who do not spend much time in earnest prayer, are not fit to handle the work of God in any of its branches; for if they do, human depravity will surely overcome them and they will lift up their souls unto vanity. Those who become coworkers with Jesus Christ, and who have spirituality to discern spiritual things, will feel their need of virtue and of wisdom from Heaven in handling His work."[10]

Embracing the Challenge

What could God do with you, in you, through you if you transformed your life into one of prayer? Do it and find out. Experience the blessing of God's renewal, power, and growth by turning your church into a house of prayer. Pray as if your life depended on it. If you have no desire to pray, ask God to give you some.

Make prayer your habit. Get into the pattern of praying every day for your church, your children, and your spouse. Pray with friends and get an accountability prayer partner.

Pray as a ministry to the lost, choosing at least five individuals as targets of your prayer. Love them, minister to them, meet their needs. When the appropriate time comes, share your values and testimony with them and watch what God can do in their lives. Some of them will fall in love with Jesus. They will do it in answer to your prayers, your ministry, and your attractive Christian life.

Then one day you'll be walking beside the sea of glass, and someone will come to you and say, "Thank you for taking an interest in me. I am here because of you." Wouldn't that be a glorious reward?

"Rejoice evermore. Pray without ceasing. In every thing give thanks: for this is the will of God in Christ Jesus concerning you" (1 Thess. 5:16-18, KJV).

---

[1] J. H. Rutz, *The Open Church,* p. 2.

[2] A. W. Tozer, "Reflections," *Christianity Today* 29 (Dec. 13, 1985): 46.

[3] E. G. White, *Testimonies,* vol. 7, p. 194.

[4] E. G. White, *Sons and Daughters of God,* p. 280.

[5] E. G. White, *Selected Messages,* book 1, p. 121.

[6] Unknown Christian, *The Kneeling Christian* (Scotts Valley, Calif.: CreateSpace, 2009), p. 3.

[7] Samuel Hugh Moffett, in *The Power to Make Things New,* ed. Bruce Larson (Waco, Tex.: Word, 1986), pp. 130, 131.

[8] E. G. White, *Testimonies,* vol. 1, p. 434.

[9] Oswald Chambers, *My Utmost for His Highest* (Grand Rapids: Discovery Books, 1992), Jan. 6.

[10] Ellen G. White, *Testimonies to Ministers* (Mountain View, Calif.: Pacific Press, 1923), p. 169.

Chapter 7

Building a House of Prayer

The Church That Had Been

As the conference president told me about my new assignment, he described it as "a great church" and gave a long list of exciting things that had happened there. *Had* happened there, as in *the past*. It turned out that the small town church had dwindled from about 100 members down to "13 faithful souls." But when I reluctantly arrived for my first Sabbath, I didn't encounter 13 people. I saw 9. Perhaps you could count 13 if you included me, my wife, my son, and my daughter still inside of her mother!

After several months of work with absolutely no results and no sign of so much as a pulse in the body of the church, I called up a friend. "This church is incredible," I told him. "It's incredible that 20 years have passed since their last baptism. It's incredible that they have not done public evangelism in 26 years. And it is incredible that every single suggestion I make is resolutely refused."

I had proposed that we prepare a bulletin, but they protested that there were too few to warrant one. When I raised the idea of a potluck, they spurned it because they didn't like each other. They were too tired to do outreach and rejected the idea of a children's Sabbath school on the grounds, saying that there were not enough children. Everything I tried was failing, and I was close to giving up.

"Pray the prayer of John Knox," my friend said after my frustrated litany of failures. "He prayed, 'Lord, give me Scotland, or I die!'"

"But I don't want to die!" I protested. I didn't think the chances of winning over this little town were very good, especially considering the people in my church.

My friend insisted that I would not, in fact, die. "Just pray," he insisted.

The Effect of Prayer

I began to go walking in the hills above our small valley town, praying and talking to God. It was hard, though, not to be discouraged. We had hardly any people and basically no money, no energy, and no passion. My morning oatmeal was more exciting than my church! But God had a big surprise for us all.

Down in that valley lived an 80-year-old Adventist woman, Eileen, one of the faithful nine in our congregation. She was probably the least likely person to bring renewal to anything—after all, she was 80! More than that, she was a member of a dying congregation with meager resources and no enthusiasm. But Eileen began praying for her neighbor Phoebe, a 25-year-old woman who was the classic example of moral dissipation. Every day she abused drugs and alcohol, and every night she slept with a different partner. She was probably the last person in the entire town that one would ever imagine being converted.

After more than a year as their pastor, I had finally convinced the church to host an evangelistic series by promising them that if it did not work, I would never request them to do anything else ever again. "Can we get that in writing?" they asked. They were serious.

Opening night arrived, and so did all nine of the regulars— plus one! Earlier that week on a hunting trip, disoriented by drugs, Eileen's neighbor Phoebe had accidentally shot her mother. Her mother survived, but the incident greatly disturbed the daughter. Knowing that her neighbor Eileen had been praying for her, Phoebe went to her for comfort. Eileen comforted her, invited her to stay in her house, and brought her to the first night of the evangelistic series. It was there that Phoebe first heard the gospel and came forward for the altar call.

The next night the attendance included all nine of the regulars—plus 50 other people! Energized by the life-changing news about Jesus, Phoebe had phoned all her friends and relatives to attend the series. God kept surprising us, and by the end of the meeting 10 people had accepted baptism, more than doubling the size of the church! God's blessings continued, and the last time I was at that church, so were 137 other people—not including any unborn children this time!

The prayers of an 80-year-old woman ignited a radical change in Phoebe's life and that of the church. Eileen didn't have much energy, much money, or many outstanding talents, but God worked mightily in answer to her prayers. When I had preached on the importance of prayer, eight people in the church smiled politely and did nothing. But Eileen prayed! She caught the vision, acted on her conviction, and prayed for Phoebe, never imagining the awesome results that would follow.

Church renewal comes not by wishing, by hoping, by complaining, or even by working hard. It results as an answer to prayer. We have not yet learned this lesson. While we know that prayer is important, we don't understand that it is critical. As much as we talk about our need for prayer, we are still woefully ignorant of its power in our churches and in our lives.

Three Churches

All churches operate from one of three distinct models of prayer and spirituality. We might label the first model the Prayerless Church. Prayer may occur in such a church, but it places only casual emphasis on prayer. The Prayerless Church probably has a weekly prayer meeting and offers prayer at the beginning and end of every program, at the start and close of Sabbath school, and at least an invocation and benediction during the Sabbath morning worship service. However, such prayers are there because it's the way things are supposed to be done—it's listed in the bulletin.

A Prayerless Church

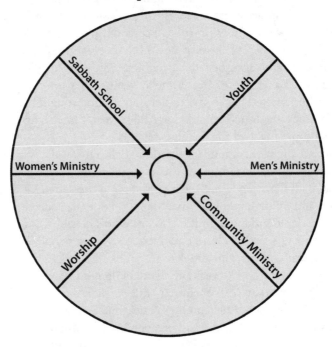

Then there is the Church With Prayer. It has decided that prayer is important enough that it has delegated the prayer ministry to a group of people called prayer warriors. So prayer emerges as one of the ministries of the church. Though it emphasizes prayer to some degree, the congregation at large has no sense of urgency about prayer. Most of the members of a Church With Prayer don't really do that much praying—they believe that someone else will do it.

A Church With Prayer

The third model is the Church of Prayer. Taking the Holy Spirit and prayer very seriously, it puts them at the center of every activity. Such congregations not only pray at the beginning and end of every meeting, but make sure that all the activities of the church are bathed with the aroma of prayer and the power of the Holy Spirit. The atmosphere and culture of the church is all about prayer. Thus the church becomes a house of prayer.

Such houses of prayer become sanctuaries of connectedness with God. The board meeting will turn into a prayer meeting, while prayer meeting itself offers a time of commitment and celebration. The members of the church recognize their need of the Spirit and cry out to God, "We are helpless without You!" They passionately seek Him.

I travel extensively conducting seminars on prayer, church growth, and spirituality. As I visit new places and meet new people, I like to ask them which type of church they belong to. The majority is definitely in the category of Church With Prayer (maybe 80 percent of Adventist churches fall into that category). Another 15 percent acknowledge that their church is a Prayerless Church, and only 5 percent say that their church is a Church of Prayer.

A Church of Prayer

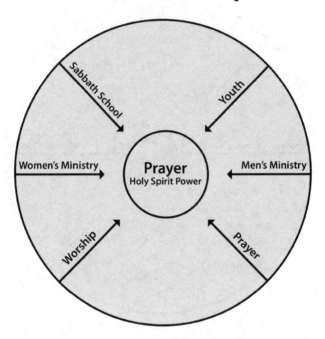

Ninety-five percent of our churches relate to prayer as an incidental concern or as the ministry of a few people. Thus 95 percent of Adventist congregations need to move from treating prayer as a formality or one ministry among many and become sanctuaries focused on the God of answered prayers. How can a church become a church of prayer?

One of the most important things you can do for the cause of God is to pray for your churches, members, community, and at least five people you would like to bring to the lord.

Building a House of Prayer

1. Establish a praying leadership. First, the key leaders of a church (especially the pastor and the first tier of leadership) must buy into prayer as the only option, and they must exercise prayer both as individuals and as a leadership team. They must love God and have an authentic walk with Him. Their lives must reflect an utter dependency upon God. Then those leaders must start praying for their church and for the emergence of a group of passionate Christians who believe the same. In every church you will find a group of people who really recognize the importance of prayer—the leaders must be just those type of people. Only praying leaders build a praying church.

2. Instill the vision. The top leaders and all Sabbath school teachers must instill the vision for prayer using every possible means. Sermons, testimonies, stories, Sabbath school, slogans—use any means available to reinforce the message that everything depends upon prayer and that God will do great things in answer to our petitions. Such an effort will require creative repetition to maintain the freshness of the message and yet still keep it before the people at all times. Employ as many different methods as available to inspire and motivate the congregation to connect with God and to rely on Him.

The key to instilling the vision for prayer successfully is getting every leader of every department to buy into it. Under their leadership prayer must infuse their departments and their ministries. Every week Sabbath school teachers must emphasize the importance of prayer. Elders must stress the importance of prayer to those they minister to in Bible study, visitation, hospitality, and administration. All deacons and deaconesses should do the same in their areas of service until every interaction and every activity centers on prayer. Everyone in a position of leadership and ministry must be a source of inspiration to motivate people to connect with God and to pray more.

The role of the pastor and the key leaders, therefore, is to encourage the congregation to pray, but specific focus needs to be on the first tier of leadership. Those leaders in turn must also inspire the congregation, but particularly those in the second tier of leadership. The leaders continue to instill the vision using every opportunity available to them until most people in the church have been taught and motivated to pray.

At the beginning process people will respond with some enthusiasm: "We love what we are hearing." It takes about two years to reach the next stage: resistance. That is when members start expressing that they're tired of the constant emphasis. "We need to move on to another subject!" The church will remain at this stage for about a year or two, but do not give up! Do not relax the stress on prayer and the Holy Spirit. The third stage is the most important. Now people begin to say, "Prayer is what we're all about." In all, it might require four or five years to reach this point, but it is worth it. Now the church is a house of prayer! Many pastors and leaders lose heart before they get here, but keep praying. God will bless you, and eventually your church will become filled with prayer and the Holy Spirit, an open theater in which God will display His love and power.

3. Teach the people how to pray. Most Christian prayers are connected to a wish list. "Lord, bless me, bless my family. God, give me this or that." It is imperative that the spiritual leaders of the church instruct the congregation how to have a meaningful hour with God every day. Explain to them that prayer is about adoration and praise, enjoying the presence of God, asking for forgiveness and victory over sin, seeking the conversion of unsaved people, and expressing thanksgiving and supplication for the needs of oneself, one's family, and one's church.

Show people how to have meaningful daily worship, as well as family worship and corporate worship. In every case make it personal, touch the heart, and pray for people and their needs. When an answer to prayer takes place, highlight it up front in church, reminding everyone that God is working among them.

Then help them to understand why God does not answer some prayers. Here is a simple formula that may help with some of our struggles about seemingly unanswered prayer.

When the request is wrong, God says, "No."

When the timing is wrong, God says, "Slow."

When you are wrong, God says, "Grow."

When everything's right, God says, "Let's go!"

4. Keep it going. After a while any project or emphasis in the church will lose its luster. People's initial enthusiasm will wane, and they'll stop praying with the intensity that they had before. I have seen this everywhere. Members start strong in prayer with much of the congregation praying, but eventually interest diminishes. Here are some reasons churches lose their zeal for prayer.

- The emphasis on prayer has faded, and with it has gone the sense of urgency.
- Those with the gift of intercessory prayer get delegated the responsibility to pray, exempting the rest of the church.
- Formality replaces the sense of the supernatural.
- Tracking the results of prayer has become less common.
- Prayer has become disconnected from the worship experience.
- The prayer emphasis has shifted away from the needs of the unchurched and dechurched, and increasingly toward those of the congregation.
- The link between prayer and evangelism gradually gets ignored.

I first discovered this pattern in my initial attempts to emphasize prayer. At the beginning of the first year of my prayer focus I presented eight sermons on the topic of prayer, and people discussed it everywhere and all the time. One of the sermons I preached was on intercessory praye, in which I emphasized praying and ministering to other people. About two weeks later a woman from the congregation came to tell me that that sermon had changed her life. A few years previous she had had a falling out with another church member after many years of close friendship. As a result they had not had any contact whatsoever in the past two and a half years. Then, she reported, she began to implement my recommendations for intercessory prayer, and the Lord put in her heart a conviction that she should pray for her former friend. At first she resisted, but eventually she had to surrender to the Spirit. He began to soften her heart toward the other woman, and she went to her and they reconciled.

For a time I heard story after story like this one from many people in the congregation. By July and August, however, they had ceased. It dawned on me that there hadn't been much emphasis on prayer for the past four months. I decided at that time that almost every week, in one way or another, I would stress prayer by my preaching, through testimonies shared with the congregation, in stories—in any way that I could.

Along with that public emphasis, I began to pray that God would do something extraordinary in our midst. One year we prayed for 30 baptisms, and the Lord gave us 36. The second year when we prayed for 50, God blessed us with 57. Another year when we prayed for 100 baptisms, God brought 99. One year we were in desperate straits: we needed $130,000 or the fire marshal would shut us down, because the church building was too large to continue operating without a firewall. In that year the Lord provided all $130,000—an impossible goal. Such things really helped my congregation to see the activity of God in their midst.

Pray that God will do spectacular things among you. Pray for large numbers of baptisms. Pray to retire debt. Pray for a new building. Pray for what you know that you could never do apart from God's powerful Spirit. Always ask God to do great things. I know that He will.

"Keep your wants, your joys, your sorrows, your cares, and your fears before God. You cannot burden Him; you cannot weary Him. . . . Take to Him everything that perplexes the mind. Nothing is too great for Him to bear, for He holds up worlds, He rules over all the affairs of the universe. Nothing that in any way concerns our peace is too small for Him to notice. There is no chapter in our experience too dark for Him to read; there is no perplexity too difficult for Him to unravel."*

5. Provide many opportunities for prayer. In our fast-moving age and society of swamped schedules, to put all of the prayer emphasis on one time or place is a mistake. Most churches measure the effectiveness of their prayer ministry by how many people come on Tuesday or Wednesday nights, but these days it is difficult for people to get to church for a midweek service at a particular time. It is necessary, therefore, to provide multiple times and places for people to pray and connect with God.

Some groups may meet at 7:00 or 8:00 on Sabbath morning to pray. Many congregations have prayer opportunities after church for anyone who would like to pray or have other people pray for them. Prayer can take place during Sabbath school, small groups can be praying units, and the church should consider offering various times during the week for people to pray: Sunday morning, Tuesday noon, Thursday evening—any time

Practical Steps

1. Pray for a hungering and thirsting after God.

2. Ask God to give others a burden for prayer. Then identify a group of praying people who can provide leadership in a prayer movement.

3. Appoint a prayer coordinator or prayer director in the church who will plan, program, and manage times of prayer. Such an individual's main task is to keep the vision of prayer in front of the people.

4. Promote prayer in connection with projects of the church, such as ministries, events, the work of the local Adventist school, and evangelistic series.

5. Regularly publish and distribute a church prayer list.

6. Emphasize intercessory prayer for unsaved people. Aim to have at least 50 percent of your congregation praying for others.

7. Have more than one prayer meeting. Develop a whole program of prayer meetings according to ages, agencies, tasks, and needs (prayer for the sick, a ministry to Jewish people, men and women in the armed forces, college students, missionaries, etc.).

8. Plan interesting and special programs with a special emphasis on prayer. Some ideas are:

• Hold a prayer conference in your church.

• Provide two or three prayer retreats each year.

• Host a prayer banquet.

• At least once a year, preach a series on prayer.

• Offer a small group Bible study or Sabbath school class on prayer.

• Establish a men's and women's prayer breakfast group that will meet for prayer every month.

• Schedule, during the corporate worship hour, testimonies about prayer every two or three weeks.

that fits the needs of your community. Use the church building as well as homes, restaurants, parks, bookstores, and coffee shops—even the marketplace, if possible.

6. Emphasize intercessory prayer for the unsaved. If the church is going to reach its community and experience true kingdom growth, it must be intentional about intercessory prayer. Challenge the congregation to pray for their unsaved loved ones. Every believer must pray for, minister to, and actively love at least five to 10 people every day. Through the power of God and the influence of friendship, several of them will come to the Lord and into His church.

7. Emphasize victory through prayer. Victory over sin or the evil one is impossible without serious prayer. It is hopeless to try to live the wonderful Christian life without power from above. Prevailing in life is really prevailing in prayer. Many Christians do not enjoy such a life because they do not pray enough.

But prevailing in prayer is God's will for us. To prevail is to be successful in the face of difficulty, to completely dominate, to overcome and triumph. Prevailing prayer is prayer that pushes right through all difficulties and obstacles, drives back all the opposing forces of Satan, and secures the will of God in the world. Such prayer not only takes the initiative but continues on the offensive for God until spiritual victory is won. An army marches on its feet, but the church of the living God marches on its knees.

In our interviews with pastors one of them encapsulated his role as the key leader of the church this way: "During the week I talk to God about my congregation, but on Sabbath I talk to my congregation about God." Another pastor concluded that the heart of pastoral work was to pray and help the congregation to pray. Still another one said that his role was bringing men and women, boys and girls, to God through the power of prayer. And yet another one stated that the role of leadership was to turn the church into a house of prayer for all people.

I challenge you to evaluate your role as a leader of any kind of ministry and as a member in light of the power of prayer. I urge you to respond to God, to get to know Him. It will require effort, prioritizing, even some sacrifice on your part—but no effort will be more richly rewarded than the work done on our knees. Go forward, then, in prayer!

★ E. G. White, *Steps to Christ,* p. 100.

Section 4:

Committed and Active Laity

Real growth in the church takes place when members are passionate about the mission of Jesus Christ and are active in sharing His love with the world around them. However, we discovered from our research that 66 percent of our members have not won one person to Jesus in their lifetime. Lack of member involvement in evangelism could result from weak spirituality, lack of vision, fear of rejection, busyness, disdain of traditional methods of evangelism (such as door-to-door and other public methods), a professionalizing of evangelism, or doubt that people are interested in the gospel and particularly in our unique message. Some people may even be embarrassed by their local church. This section attempts to reverse this trend.

It has four chapters.

1. "The Missing Ingredient in Most Churches"
2. "The Most Effective Evangelist in the World"
3. "Chain Reaction: *Oikos* Evangelism"
4. "Dying for Change: The Challenges We Face Today"

The first chapter deals with the internal motivation for witnessing. Most Christians do not engage in evangelism because they have very little of this factor. Read the chapter and see how much of it you have and what you can do to have more of it and then help others to do the same.

The second chapter answers the question "Who is the most effective evangelist in the world?" The answer might surprise you.

The third chapter is about the biblical principle of *oikos* and how that is the heart of evangelism. It is also the most effective form of evangelism.

The last chapter deals with some disturbing trends that we found from several surveys we conducted on Sabbath morning in many Seventh-day Adventist churches. The heart of the chapter is about the changes that we need to make the church healthy and growing. This shift can take place only when everyone in the church cooperates with each other.

Chapter 8

The Missing Ingredient
in Most Churches

A friend of mine told me about an argument she had had with her husband last week. They were on their way to a family luncheon to celebrate his sister's fortieth birthday and had agreed before church that they
would stay for the benediction, shake a few hands, and then leave quickly
so as not to be late. As they got into the car to head to lunch, he lightly
chided her: "Honey, it's 12:44! You said we would leave quickly today."

She protested, "But we only stayed 14 minutes after the benediction.
That's not long at all. Besides, we both love this church—you know it's
hard to leave!"

My friend and her husband belong to a congregation that they love, a
place they are so enthusiastic about that they drive 45 minutes to worship
there every Sabbath, and 45 minutes for board meetings and baby showers
and Bible study. And they don't go all that way because there are no churches
closer to their home. They commute that distance and come early and stay
late because they are committed to its members. They have a loving community there, they have fun there, and they are excited to go to church.

In our interviews of members of thriving churches we noticed that
healthy, growing congregations have a special ingredient that plateauing
and declining congregations do not. That ingredient is *enthusiasm,* and
most churches don't have enough of it. In this chapter I am using the
words "enthusiasm" and "excitement" as synonymous. Enthusiasm is simply faith in action. A logical expression of a joyful knowledge of God's
good news for the world, it is born out of love and adoration for the Lord
and spills over into our passion for sharing Him with the world around us.

The members of growing churches are excited about God, excited
about their church, and excited to share their faith with others. They are
proud of their local congregation and eager to bring with them their
friends and relatives, knowing that they'll be blessed. For these people,
going to church is a joyful experience that they want to share with others.

When the church growth movement was in its infancy, Donald

McGavran's book *The Bridges of God*, which launched the concept, said it well: the best explanation of church growth is the enthusiasm of people about God and their congregation. That was 50 years ago, and it is still the same today.[1] When I asked pastors of thriving Adventist churches about the secret of growth in their congregations, they told me that it was the enthusiasm of the people: they were excited about their church and recommended it to their friends.

Seven Factors of an Enthusiastic Church Culture

What causes such excitement? Our findings tell us that at least seven factors contribute to a culture of people enthusiastic about their church.

1. The experience of the gospel. When people fall in love with Jesus, they develop a sense of joy, meaning, and excitement. As we feel God's presence, it thrills the heart, and we desire to do whatever He asks. People who love Jesus have traveled all over the world to tell others about Him. They have risked hardship, persecution, and difficulty. Some have even given their lives for His sake. The gospel inspires and motivates us to share Him with the world around us.

2. Buying into a cause. As human beings we long to be a part of something larger than ourselves, to know that we are making an important difference in the world. And as Christians we recognize the kingdom of God as our cause, and our work for that kingdom makes an eternal difference in lives of others. Whatever we do in the service of God—teach a Sabbath school class, visit shut-ins, minister to those who are homeless, lead in worship, give a Bible study—we do it to glorify God and bring hope, grace, the presence of God, and eternity to others. Enthusiastic congregations know the significance of their ministries.

3. Love and acceptance. A spirit of love, acceptance, and forgiveness permeates the whole church. Both those in the congregation and those outside of it will experience that love. A feeling of belonging and intimacy suffuses the place. People can express their views without condemnation even if they're different from those of others. They know that although they might dress differently, eat differently, and look differently, they are still accepted and loved. Growing churches major in the major issues, which are loving God and people.

4. A warm and joyous climate. An atmosphere of love and acceptance leads to a climate of warmth and joy, affection and happiness. The research studies Valuegenesis 1 and 2 show that the most important expectation that young people have of their church is for it to have a warm and loving environment. They want to belong a place where they are loved and accepted, challenged and yet feel safe.

5. God-exalting worship. Members of an enthusiastic congregation look forward to going to church because they know that God is going to show up and bless them and do great things among them. Later on I will devote a whole chapter to the experience of God-exalting and God-honoring worship

6. Meaningful and relevant ministries. Thriving congregations conduct everything they do from a sense of spirituality and care. From Sabbath school to children's ministries, from community outreach to nurture, the ministries of the church should be meaningful and relevant. The church makes a concentrated and all-out intentional effort to meet the total needs of the believer and the seeker.

7. A sense of excellence.[2] Successful churches constantly seek to do everything possible to honor God and to inspire people. Members can feel good about their ministries because they are done well, and they can feel comfortable about inviting their friends and family, knowing that what the church does is something to be proud of.

How is your church doing in this area? Does it have a sense of excitement and joy? Are members enthusiastic enough about their experience with Christ and the people in the congregation to share that experience with others?

Of course, you may have some questions for me, too. Chances are that your church could use a little more joy and excitement. "Sure!" you say. "But how? What other miracle do you want me to perform?"

I admit that excitement is difficult to manufacture, because it has to do with the total quality of experience in church; but it is still an important factor in getting a church growing and then sustaining that growth. Although developing an enthusiastic congregation might be difficult, it is not impossible. With the blessing of God and with intentionality, it can be done.

Ten Ways to Build Enthusiasm

To have a growing, happy church that will bring glory to God and lead people into His kingdom, you must develop the seven features of an enthusiastic church culture in your own congregation. Moving from principles to praxis, what steps can you take to begin establishing those seven characteristics within your church family? Here are 10 possible ways to nurture them within your community of faith. It is a compilation of what we saw growing churches do to generate enthusiasm.

1. Pray. A wellspring of joy, love, faith, and expectation will develop as you pray. Pray that God will bring a great sense of excitement and victory to your life and to those of your people that will spill over into the public services. Whoever you are, prayer is for you.

2. Embrace spirituality. The more spiritual the people are, the more excited they are about God and the church and the more they are inclined to share their faith with others. Those who love God will do anything to honor Him and glorify Him. As a result, they are those in the forefront of ministry and evangelism. Therefore, your ministry to develop a healthy, Christ-centered spiritual life feeds right into the general culture of joy and enthusiasm in your church.

3. Promote faith-based optimism. This sparks anticipation, it supports joy, and it overcomes trouble. We're talking not about spiritual hype but about developing a positive mental attitude. Even though some consider certain elements of positive thinking as secular or humanistic, we are talking about faith-based hope and optimism that works because God is behind it. If you think you can, you're right: God will make it possible. But if you think you can't, you're right still. You won't be able to do it without God's help.

The most profound concept I learned from our research is that the mind is like a field. It will grow anything you plant in it. Should you plant weeds in a field, it will grow weeds. The same applies to corn, cotton, or anything else. And it is equally true of the mind. If you sow negative thoughts, that is what you will reap. But if you sow positive thoughts, you will reap the same.

Helping people embrace a faith-based optimism is one of your tasks as a spiritual leader. As individuals think in their hearts, so are they (Prov. 23:7, NKJV)! Ask and you will receive; seek and you will find; knock and it will be opened to you (Matt. 7:7, 8; Luke 11:9, 10). It may not guarantee health, wealth, or fame (as some may claim), but it does point toward a balanced approach to life. Nor does it ignore the fact that the world contains sorrow, heartache, sin, disease, and pain. Rather, it means recognizing those problems while believing that God will enable us to rise above them. Happiness in life is largely a matter of attitude. Millionaires are often miserable, while others who have barely enough to buy groceries may be radiantly happy. Faith-based optimism is essential to creating excitement, and when leaders stand to lead, they must be positive. Such faith-based optimism should influence everything in the church all the way from ministry to preaching, from witnessing to life.

It was a lesson that I began to learn in my first pastorate. I would hear sometimes that I wasn't feeding the people. But that made no sense to me, because I knew I was preaching the gospel. I was into Paul like you wouldn't believe, and I thought I was doing a good job! What were my critics talking about?

Then one day I was sitting in my office and questioning myself: "Will this sermon help anyone? Will it encourage anyone? Will it lift someone up?" When I began building my sermons around those criteria, I discovered immediately the difference they made. During my first pastorate I had said in effect to the people, "You brood of vipers! Who warned you to flee from the coming wrath?" (Matt. 3:7; Luke 3:7). I didn't realize how negative my previous approach was, how devoid of positive encouragement. Figuratively, people came crawling into church. Having been beaten down by the world, they were almost ready to give up. They looked at me as if to say, "Preacher, do you have a good word for me today? Does God have anything to say to me about this mess I'm living in? Do you have any words of hope and encouragement to lift up my spirit?"

Learning my lesson, I began to preach on such texts as "My grace is sufficient for you, for my power is made perfect in weakness" (2 Cor. 12:9). Some may be tempted to charge that I compromised, that I stopped presenting the whole gospel. No, I still preached on sin and holiness, on humanity's lost condition, and on judgment. I still spoke on commitment and self-denial, but not all the time and not in the same way. And every Sabbath I asked myself those same questions to test the helpfulness of my sermons.

Before I had admonished people to be better and to work harder for the Lord. Now I began saying to them, "It's wonderful to serve God. He knows all about your situation, and He will give you the strength to face it." Again and again I told the members that God loves them and is crazy about them. That's what I mean by radiating optimism from the pulpit. Accentuate the positive.

The principles I learned can apply to anyone. Whether as pastors, Sabbath school teachers, or anyone else, you can make a difference if you minister with enthusiasm, authenticity, and relevancy. Put them into practice in preaching and teaching, in ministry and evangelism. Whoever you do, do it all for the glory of God.

4. Minister with enthusiasm. It lifts people's spirits and is catching. Be genuine, but be enthusiastic. I learned from pastors of growing churches that when you're going to the pulpit, you should get there in a hurry and act as if it's worth being there. Often I see pastors trudge to the pulpit as though they dreaded it. If you're going to create excitement, you must be enthusiastic and speak with passion.

"That's just not me," you protest. Then be as enthusiastic as you can be. Enthusiasm comes as a result of knowing how Jesus loves us and that His love drove Him all the way to the cross to die for us. People get excited about sports or money or children or controversial subjects at board meetings. How much more should we be enthusiastic over Jesus, who valued our lives by the worth of His own life.

Phineas F. Bresee declared, "If any man loses his enthusiasm, he might as well be buried." He knew that a lack of enthusiasm "is one of the greatest hindrances to the work of God." Furthermore, he even said that a lack of enthusiasm "is sure evidence that the heavenly vision is dim."[3] Some people consider enthusiasm a worldly and insincere emotion. Actually, the opposite is true. The two Greek words from which we derive the English "enthusiasm" mean "*God inside you.*"[4] What better source of enthusiasm is there than God inside you? The truth is that enthusiasm is simply faith in action. It is the logical expression of the joyful knowledge of God's good news for the world.

5. Set realistic goals of faith. A goal gives people something to get excited about, something to work toward and look forward to. Most people want to attempt something great, and they will get excited about the possibility of achieving it. A good goal will require special effort and divine help. While it should be bigger than the resources that you presently see that you have, if it is impossible it will discourage people.

6. Spiritualize the work of the church. In all your communication, make it clear that saving souls and rebuilding lives is what the role of the church is all about. Whether from the pulpit and in newsletters, in phone calls and board meetings, constantly remind people that you are not just increasing numbers or erecting buildings—you are doing God's work. Every ministry is about leading people to Jesus and making an eternal difference in their lives.

Read the newsletters of exciting churches, and you will discover that everything is spiritually oriented. They don't just raise money—they ask their people to make a great gift to God. Nor are they merely constructing a building—they are a providing a place for people who are going to be won as a result of faithful stewardship. Church leaders could say, "You owe 10 percent of your income to the Lord and you ought to give another 5 percent to help us do some of the things we're trying to do." But people would complain and protest that they couldn't do it—too many of their own bills to pay. Suppose the church leadership says instead, "Giving is about your love and allegiance to God. God is doing wonderful things in the world, and by giving you can be part of that. Giving is about your love for God and the priorities of your life. We're doing a great work for God, and you have a chance to share in this tremendous ministry. You can make an investment in the kingdom of God." People will respond much differently. They will invest their resources into a vision like that.

When visiting one growing Adventist church, I met a dentist who loved God and his church and community deeply and passionately. I asked him about his ministry in the church. He informed me that he was in charge of the audio system in his church. Then he got excited and started to tell about all the things he does so that the audio system operates effectively. "I come here to the church several times every week to check on the equipment and make sure it works properly, because what happens here on Sabbath morning is a matter of life and death." Pausing, he said, "No, no, it is a matter of *eternal* life and death." The Holy Spirit had opened the eyes of this dentist to the eternally significant consequences of his ministry in the audio booth on Sabbath mornings. I pray that all of us could see that we do not just teach a Sabbath school class or lead in the Pathfinders ministry or distribute food to the needy, but are making an eternal difference in the life of those we touch.

The Bible says to do everything to the glory of God. If you can't relate the purpose of something as furthering His honor and praise, then you shouldn't be doing it in the first place!

7. Celebrate victories and successes. This is vital for building up excitement and godly enthusiasm. Every time someone gets saved, give it special attention in the church service. Or whenever someone has an answer to prayer that is significant, report it in a public meeting and in the church newsletter. Help the people to feel that something is happening at their church, that something wonderful is going on all the time. You don't have to make things up—just point out what God is doing in your midst. In the thriving churches that we studied we found them celebrating baptisms and baby dedications, generous giving and healthy growth, victories and successes. Many even show a video at the end of the year highlighting all that God has done in their midst.

8. Focus on people's needs and help them. I would venture that most of those attending your church would be impressed if they knew that it was actually helping people, whether it was by providing meals, giving them clothes, or assisting them through their personal problems. Here is where love, acceptance, and forgiveness are vital. While you don't have to condone their problems or their sins, you do need to love people. You do need to accept them just as they are, and you do need to forgive them for their wrongdoings. When you focus on meeting people's needs, you'll discover that even those who never want the church to do anything but preach the gospel will be impressed that their church is really aiding people.

9. Plan outstanding programs. We have 52 Sabbath morning services and 52 Wednesday night services wherein we do about the same things with the same people—just fewer and fewer of them as time passes. That can get boring. So plan some outstanding programs, introduce variety, challenge the people to get others involved in doing something different. People would comment that in my churches the services were never the same twice. Not everyone can handle variety, but do something to give the people a feeling of expectancy.

One way to encourage excitement is to bring in renowned guest speakers and special music artists from time to time. It gives the sense that something special and worthwhile is happening. You may have to grow in membership before you can incorporate such opportunities into your program in any significant measure, but you will need to do it to maintain excitement in your church.

10. Develop inspiring worship services. That doesn't necessarily require an emotional response in the form of outward demonstration, but worshippers should feel something. It must fit your personality, and it has to reflect that of your people. Also it should fall within the limits of your resources. If you have someone who can "sing the glory down," great! If not, utilize the various strengths within the congregation and do something else.

Surely you can implement one or two of the above suggestions to help build enthusiasm in your local church. It will be worth your best efforts. As the church becomes more joyous and positive, more people will be won to the Lord, and nothing is so exciting as seeing people coming to your church and committing themselves to Jesus.

Ultimately, excitement emerges when people feel the love of God and His grace extending to them and through them to others. When the church is truly a safe and warm place, the result will be enthusiasm. Members will enjoy being there, will be eager to invite others, and will be willing to do more ministries.

In studying the differences between growing churches and declining ones, we concluded that the members of the latter tend to be neutral or even ashamed of their church. In contrast, the members of the thriving congregations are proud of where they worship and fellowship, approve of their pastor, and are eager for Sabbath school and worship services. Ultimately, they are proud of God, the one who is doing something extraordinary right in their midst.

My Car and My Excitement

A few years ago my wife needed a car. So one day we went out looking for that perfect vehicle that was only 1 year old, had less than 10,000 miles, was loaded with every option, and yet cost less than $5,000. Well, we did not find that car, but we did discover a beautiful Toyota Camry that was only 4 years old with most of the necessary features. My wife liked the vehicle, and I went in to ask the dealer about the price. "This car is a steal," he told me. "It is only 4 years old and has a little bit more than 100,000 miles, but mostly highway miles. I will sell it to you below book—only $9,998."

"Thank you, but I do not have $10,000," I replied. "We only have a little more than $4,000." He offered to finance it for us, but we told him that we always pay cash for every purchase that we make.

As we were walking out, he called us back and told us to wait, explaining that he would talk with his manager. About 20 minutes later he came out, saying, "My boss is crazy. He is willing to sell the car for $8,000."

"We do not have $8,000—only $4,000."

"Mr. Kidder, I cannot sell you this car for $4,000. It is worth more than $10,000. But let me go to the boss again and see what we can do." Twenty minutes later he returned. "The boss must love you. He is willing to sell you the car for $7,000." Again I told him that we only had $4,000. This went back and forth from 11:00 a.m. till 7:00 p.m. A little after 7:00 I drove the car off the lot after I had paid him about $5,000.

Let me tell you, I was excited! I had gotten a great deal and told the story to everyone I knew, sharing it in all my classes, and even building a sermon around it. In fact, I related it so many times that I noticed people starting to avoid me: they knew that talking to me meant that they'd hear about the car again.

If a deal of $5,000 made me so excited and willing to repeat it a thousand times, how much more eternal life! At the cross of Calvary Jesus gave me the deal of a life filled with joy, purpose, and hope today, and He added eternity on top of it. When we realize what Jesus has done for us, we will center our lives on Him and tell the world His story with all the zeal and enthusiasm that we have.

---

[1] Quoted by Bill M. Sullivan, *Ten Steps to Breaking the 200 Barrier* (Kansas City, Mo.: Beacon Hill, 1988), p. 73.

[2] I will be dealing in more details with this subject in the chapter "The Worship Experience Your Heart Longs For."

[3] In Sullivan, p. 73.

[4] *Ibid.*

Chapter 9

The Most Effective Evangelist
in the World

In my training seminars in church growth and evangelism I often start with the question Who is the most effective evangelist in the world? I always get the same predictable answers: Doug Batchelor, Walter Pearson, Mark Finley, Alejandro Bullòn, Dwight Nelson, Kenneth Cox, etc. Then when I ask how people come to the Lord and the church, I usually get some wildly different answers. Putting up a list of methods, I have the class suggest what they believe is the percentage of people who come to the Lord and the church as a result of each approach. For example:

- special needs (such as illness, divorce, loneliness, loss of a job, etc.)
- walk-ins (people who live nearby and visit uninvited)
- pastor
- door-to-door visitation
- Sabbath school
- public evangelistic meetings
- church programs (health seminars, VBS, school, Pathfinders, etc.)

Most of the people agree that 90 percent of the people in the church are there because of felt needs. Others insist that visitation brings in another 60 percent. Still others say that the pastor brings in at least 40 to 60 percent. Many more believe that public evangelism produces 50 to 90 percent.

Well, who is the most effective evangelist in the world? The research may surprise you.

In the autumn of 2004 a survey went to a sample of Seventh-day Adventist congregations in the North American Division to be given to attending members on a certain Sabbath. The purpose of the survey was to discover their devotional and evangelistic practices. How do Adventist Christians fare in evangelism? The 1,689 surveys told us. The key features of the data appear below and in the following chapters. We need to pay attention to the information given to us by these 1,689 Adventists, because if we can understand what is happening and why, then we can improve the way that we do church and the manner that we reach out to people in Jesus' name.

The Demographics

First, a look at the composition of the respondents may be helpful. As to gender, 57 percent were female—quite typical for Adventist congregations. The sample consists mostly of longtime Adventists: 61 percent had been members for more than 20 years, and another 15 percent had been in the church from 11 to 20 years. Only about 4 percent had been members less than a year. Not only that, but 60 percent had grown up with an Adventist parent. All this seems to indicate two things: the power of relationships in bringing people to the church, and that our congregations are not bringing in many new members who have no Adventist background or who come from outside our community of faith.

The data, moreover, indicate an aging church. More than 60 percent were more than 45 years of age, with 22 percent being 65 or older. Only about 9 percent were under 25. Such data show the need for the church to be much more intentional about reaching and keeping young people.

How They Joined

A topic of special interest included in the 2004 survey was a question asking the relative strength of nine factors in influencing the respondents to join the Adventist Church. We have combined the percentages of those who reported "quite a bit of influence" and "very great influence."

How People Join the Church

	Percentage
brought up in an Adventist home	59
a friend or relative	58
read books, journals, other material	49
public evangelism meetings	36
Bible studies in the home	34
visits by a pastor	20
television or radio programs	20
Bible correspondence course	19
material on the Internet	7
others	22

The only significant new item that emerged in the "others" category was Christian education and Adventist schoolteachers.

The Most Effective Evangelist in the World!

Back to my seminars. Up on the screen I put a list of various methods used to bring people to the Lord, and the audience often offers wildly different guesses about the effectiveness of each one. Then when I show them the results of this study, they are shocked. Most people start questioning the findings. I usually hear some protesting, "This cannot be true. Felt needs is how people come to the Lord." Others say, "No, no, public evangelism is how people accept Jesus." Another group believes that the pastor and church programs are what really work.

But maybe their church is the exception. Just to be sure, I go through the list one by one, asking them to stand up when I read the primary influence in their conversion to the Lord and church. Whether the crowd is small, medium size, or very large; whether it is in big churches or small ones; whether it is in rural, suburban, or city churches, I always get a similar result.

special needs	2-5 percent
walk-in	2-5 percent
pastor	2-5 percent
visitation	2-5 percent
Sabbath school	2-5 percent
evangelistic series	2-5 percent

Now I add:

friends/relatives	70-95 percent

That's when people experience the "Aha!" moment. They start saying, "Well, yes, my mom had the most influence on my religious experience," or "My neighbor took me to Sabbath school when I was a little girl." Another person might add, "My grandmother was an Adventist, and she prayed for me for years. Finally I decided to take God seriously." Someone else remembers that it was a coworker who invited him to church so many years ago.

The figure I get for the influence of moms and dads, friends or relatives, neighbors or coworkers is usually between 70 and 95 percent. Then I go back and ask them the same question I started with: "Who is the most effective evangelist in the world?" Now the answer is unanimous. It is obvious from both the formal research and the informal data collected in such groups that the most effective evangelist in the world is the one who takes personal interest in us and shares Jesus in a wholistic and attractive way. Again I repeat my question: "Who is the most effective evangelist in the world?" The answer I get now is "*I* am the most effective evangelist in the world."

The Adventist study is consistent with all similar research. Win Arn[1] and Thom Rainer[2] both agree that friendship is God's preferred means of reaching people. And the implications are universal in its scope. I travel all over the world, training people in evangelism and church growth. Remarkably, whether I am in Asia or Africa, North, Central, or South America, Europe or Australia, the results are the same. Most people come to the Lord through the influence of a web of relationships and friendships.

The absolutely most effective way of reaching people for the gospel is through personal influence. So what does God do? For example, how does He reach police officers? By disguising full-time ministers as police officers. Giving them the necessary gifts, passions, and credentials, He assigns them to police departments all over the nation. The same for construction workers. Again, after camouflaging full-time ministers as construction workers, He endows them with gifts and passions, makes them strong, and puts them to work at construction sites throughout every city. God's full-time ministers are everywhere: in classrooms and clinics, holding hammers and stethoscopes, in front of shareholders and behind the auditor's desk. We are all ambassadors of the gospel—we are all full-time ministers.

So in every city, every town, and every country, you will find there full-time ministers, differently made and differently gifted, in every business and vocation. God scatters us everywhere—like salt from a saltshaker—to suit His flavor. He salts the earth with His ministers, providing them with gifts to enable them to influence their friends, families, and coworkers.

How Do You Do It?

Here is an easy and practical 10-step strategy to help you win others to Christ.

1. Intentionally build relationships with five people every year. They should be individuals within your circle of regular contact. Far better your nearby relative, friend, coworker, or neighbor than your dear old aunt across the country.

2. Pray for them every day, asking God to intervene in their lives and to lead them to Himself. Ask the Lord to keep you faithful in your intercessory prayer and passionate about reaching them with the gospel.

3. Minister to their needs: physical, spiritual, and social. Take the time to be a true friend. Make them feel loved and special.

4. Share your values with them, such as why you do certain things and

why you don't do others, and always link everything to Jesus. Help them see that the Christian faith is not a set of rules, but a relationship with a wonderful God.

5. At the right time, offer your testimony with them. Tell them how much Jesus changed your life and how much He means to you. There is perhaps no evidence more persuasive than this.

6. Introduce them to Jesus. Tell them His story and how He is the hope of the world and the only way to God. Give them a gospel presentation.

Nurturing the New Believer

The new believer in Jesus has just experienced the most radical transformation in his or her orientation to life, social circle, habits, choices, and lifestyle. New Seventh-day Adventists have remapped their weekly calendars, reexamined their dinner plates, realigned themselves with biblical revelation, and made many other major adjustments. Such fledgling members now need a care that extends beyond giving them a towel to dry off after the baptism: they need to be nurtured and discipled, to be accepted by a new church family and provided protection from attacks outside the church and from problems inside it. The following four categories illustrate one way to visualize the basic requirements of the new member:*

- The new **faith** must be strengthened.
- New **friends** must be made.
- New **fellowship** must be provided.
- A place or role to **function** in ministry as part of church life must be nurtured.

Strengthening the new faith. Faith develops as the individual's walk with God continues and as he or she gains confidence in the new church family. Always the result of interpersonal experience, it grows best in the context of a faith community. In other words, you can help the new members' faith expand and mature by sharing your personal walk with God, modeling the Christian life, and helping them learn to feed themselves spiritually.

Making new friends. Do not underestimate this important step—it is a critical component of discipleship. In fact, the number of friends that a per-

7. At the appropriate time, invite them to church, a concert, a special program such as Easter or Christmas, an evangelistic meeting, a small group (it would be great to start one in your home), a Sabbath school class, or anything else that you may think of. This will ease them into church life and help connect them with other Adventist Christians.

8. Study the Bible with them so that they can understand the Christian faith and what it means to be a Seventh-day Adventist Christian.

9. Nurture the new believer. Disciple them. Help them to grow in the Christian faith. Become their pastor and encourager.

son has in the church has a direct correlation with the likelihood that he or she will remain a member in that community. It also offers a tremendous opportunity to members who may not feel very comfortable giving a formal Bible study—they can minister by making friends! Friendships develop as we take time to listen to each other and spend time together. Inviting new members home to dinner or out to a park or to some social activity with other believers are only some of the many ways that you can nurture them.

Providing fellowship. The secular definition of fellowship is a friendly association of people who share the same interests, a group working toward a common goal, a feeling of friendship or relatedness or connection between people. In the Christian sense fellowship may be described as the atmosphere of the Sabbath school or potluck meal or even the worship hour. A person may have friends in the church, but is he or she comfortable going to a church function with several people? Do new believers feel that they connect with them or have something in common? Do they share the same interests or values? Taking the time to be a part of a fellowship group that focuses on spiritual growth or ministry (or both) is another way of helping new members be a part of church life.

Finding a place in ministry. The sense of being needed by the church family will do much to help new membes feel they belong. Assist them to find an area of ministry that fits their personality and spiritual gifts. See that they get the training they must have to succeed. By doing this, you are discipling the new members, fulfilling the needs of the church, and accomplishing the gospel mission. You can help converts become disciples!

---

*I have taken some of these concepts from Ben Maxson, "Helping Converts Become Disciples," *Southern Tidings*, February 1987, p. 21.

10. Teach them to reach others. Reproduction is essential to the work of God.

One day you will be walking on the streets of gold, holding the hand of Jesus, and someone will come to you and say, "I am here because of you." That is worth all the investment you put into people.

The Power of Relationship and Personal Touch: Judy, Donna, Mary-Lin, and Jesus

Judy, a single mom in her mid-20s, came with her 5-year-old daughter to our church as a result of an invitation by one of our members to attend an evangelistic meeting. The young woman was eager to question everything and learn. Although she grew up Baptist, she left the church when she was 18 years old and became involved in some drugs, heavy drinking, and heavy partying. A one-night stand left her pregnant. The pregnancy woke her up. Although she started to work on improving her life, she did not meet with much success, often relapsing into her old ways.

When Judy moved to our area, she ended up living next to Donna, an authentic Christian woman from our church. Donna took the time to build a relationship with Judy, often going out of her way to meet her needs. For example, Donna spent hours listening to Judy and doing everything she could to help her escape her bouts of depression.

Our church was in the habit of having one evangelistic meeting every winter. That particular winter Judy was going through a very difficult time. Donna invited her to attend, and there she learned for the first time how special she was in the sight of God. She experienced God's presence and eventually asked for His grace and power. The power of His love transformed her. She asked many questions to learn everything she could about God. Several times after her baptism Judy faced many challenges to her newfound faith, but it was the relationship that she had with Donna and other new friends in the church that kept her strong and growing in the Lord.

Her story illustrates the power of combining personal evangelism with public evangelism. Here we see the importance of building relationships and of thorough follow-up. Judy did not have a dramatic Damascus road experience as did Paul, but she had an invitation to hear the gospel followed by a thorough process of discipleship that met her spiritual as well as emotional needs.

As a pastor I always visited the people I baptized the day after their baptism to encourage them and to recast the vision for evangelism and ministry for them. Judy was working as a manager in a grocery store when I stopped by. We walked around, and then I said to her, "Judy, let's pray and dedicate this grocery store as your place of ministry." As I started to leave with her after finishing the prayer, I noticed one of the cashiers who seemed to know Judy quite well. So I asked Judy about the woman. "That's Mary-Lin, a close friend of mine," she explained.

"God has a mandate for you to win Mary-Lin to Him, Judy," I told her. "Pray for her. Build your relationship with her. Love her." And that is exactly what Judy did. She loved her, prayed for her, and built a closer relationship with her.

The first thing she did was to invite Mary-Lin over to her house for supper on Friday night. Judy was on fire for God. Her excitement and changed life led Mary-Lin to the Lord. The two women started to study the Bible every Friday night. About two months later Mary-Lin was standing in the waters of baptism, giving a heartfelt testimony about how her friendship with Judy had made a powerful impact on her and brought her to Jesus. *Wow—the power of relationship!*.

You can be a Donna to a Judy in your life. In fact, *you* can be the most effective evangelist in the world! Is there any good reason not to start today?

"I pray that the sharing of your faith may promote the knowledge of all the good that is ours in Christ" (Philemon 6, RSV).

---

[1] Win Arn and Charles Arn, *The Master's Plan for Making Disciples* (Pasadena, Calif.: Church Growth Press, 1982), p. 43. See also W. Charles Arn, *How to Reach the Unchurched Families in Your Community* (Monrovia, Calif.: Church Growth, n.d.).

[2] Thom S. Rainer, *Surprising Insights From the Unchurched and Proven Ways to Reach Them* (Grand Rapids: Zondervan, 2002), p. 73.

Chapter 10

Chain Reaction:
Oikos Evangelism

It was July, the season for Vacation Bible School (VBS) programs, and I had just come from college to be the associate pastor in a large church in Spokane, Washington. That particular year Jane, an Adventist Christian from California, came to Spokane to visit her sister Laura. Jane wanted to bring her sister's children to our Vacation Bible School, but things did not work out. So just before returning to California, Jane asked me to visit her sister, whom she felt was receptive to the gospel. In fact, she turned out to be the ideal seeker.

I went to visit Laura and took with me Sally, a local church member. Immediately we started two Bible studies. Upstairs Sally studied with Laura and her daughter Kim. Meanwhile I was downstairs studying with Laura's other daughter, Sue, and Sue's husband, Gary. Laura and Kim were baptized in less than two months. Even while Sally was studying the Bible with Laura and Kim, Laura started to share Jesus with her son Charles, who got baptized about a month after she did.

Later Laura started a small group in her house and invited her neighbor Dee to attend. After a few meetings Dee brought her husband, Ken. A week or two later Dee asked her other neighbor, Terry, to be part of their fellowship. Dee, Ken, and Terry were all baptized about six months after Laura was. While Laura and Dee were active in sharing their faith, Sue and Gary invited their close friends Edgar and Terri to the Bible study that I was conducting. All four of them were baptized about a year later.

Laura, Kim, Sue, Gary, Charles, Dee, Ken, Terry, Edgar, and Terri: 10 living testimonies to the power of relationships. Both experience and research testify that the most effective way of reaching people for the gospel is through a natural web of relationship and family influence. The New Testament uses the Greek word *oikos* to illustrate this point. *Oikos* is literally translated as "household," and the Bible uses it to mean the influence of this natural set of relationships.* It was through *oikos* evangelism— sharing Jesus using the network of existing relationships—that 10 people came to the Lord and into His church.

The power of relationship is the power of invitation. It allows us to share our faith with our children and families, friends and neighbors, coworkerrs and acquaintances.

Imagine what would happen if you started to share your faith with people you know, those in your family and friendship group. I know that the world would be a much better place because you took the adventure of witnessing very seriously. Imagine your son and daughter in the kingdom of God, enjoying Jesus for eternity, because you were resolute about your faith. Imagine your mom and dad being with you in heaven. Imagine your friend coming to you in heaven and saying, "I am here because of you!"

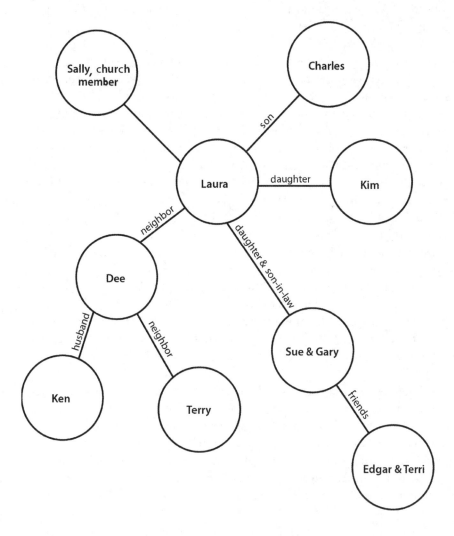

Oikos Is Biblical

What happened to Sally and Laura and me is the biblical model of spreading the gospel. The Bible is full of stories of people leading their loved ones to Jesus. Right at the beginning of John's Gospel account, he tells the story of Andrew, one of the first disciples of Jesus, bringing his brother Peter to meet the Lord (John 1:41). Then we see Philip finding Nathanael, his friend, and giving him a gospel presentation that led Nathanael also to be a follower of the Messiah (see verse 45).

See how Scripture tells the story of Andrew and Philip. "The first thing Andrew did was to find his brother Simon and tell him, 'We have found the Messiah' (that is, the Christ). . . . Philip found Nathanael and told him, 'We have found the one Moses wrote about in the Law, and about whom the prophets also wrote—Jesus of Nazareth, the son of Joseph'" (verses 41-45).

We see similar stories told again and again in the Gospels and the book of Acts. When God delivered Paul and Silas from the Philippian jail, they spoke the Word of God to the jailer and all who were in his household. The result was that the jailer "took them the same hour of the night and washed their stripes. And immediately he and all his family were baptized. Now when he had brought them into his house, he set food before them; and he rejoiced, having believed in God with all his household" (Acts 16:33, 34, NKJV). The jailer received something from Paul and Silas that compelled him to share it with his loved ones. The gospel is such wonderful news that we find ourselves compelled to bring it to others. When we understand that the stakes are sky-high (eternal life and death) and when we start experiencing the joy of salvation, our natural tendency is to tell it to those dearest to us.

Now notice how Jesus used the *oikos* principle. After He healed the demoniac, Jesus said to him, "Go home to your friends, and tell them what great things the Lord has done for you, and how He has had compassion on you" (Mark 5:19, NKJV). Jesus knew that the most persuasive witness is the testimony of a changed life shared in a natural way with those we love.

Another time, as Jesus passed by He saw Levi, the son of Alphaeus, sitting at the tax office. Jesus bade him to join Him, and Levi immediately did so. Here is the interesting thing: later on, Levi asked Jesus to dine at his house, and he also invited many fellow tax collectors to come to hear Jesus. The result was that many of them eventually followed Jesus too (Mark 2:14, 15). And in John 4, when Jesus healed the son of the nobleman, the official and his entire household believed (verse 53).

Why Is *Oikos* Effective?

Oikos—sharing faith through relationships—has such an impact because it is natural. It operates from two premises. First, when we experience Jesus and His joy, we will be compelled to share Him. Second, when our loved ones see the change in us, they will ask about it and be much more inclined to want it themselves. *Oikos* is the most efficient evangelistic approach, low in cost and high in return, often winning entire families and constantly enlarging our source of new gospel contacts. The entire process takes place in an unhurried manner and in an environment of love and acceptance, building on relationships that we already have. Your family and friends already like you and trust you, qualifications that a "professional" evangelist doesn't have. God has given you a mission field among the people that you already know.

In the previous chapter we discovered that the most effective evangelist was the person who takes a personal interest in us to share Jesus. We saw that personal influence was the most powerful human means of evangelism. In fact, we learned that some of the most successful evangelists in the world are moms and dads. Research demonstrates that when we combine "brought up in an Adventist home," "brought in by friends and relatives," and "Bible study in the home," the percentage who join is 70-80 percent. The facts are clear: most people come to the Lord and His church through personal influence in relationships. More good news: when we win people to the Lord through existing relationships, new members have a built-in, personal connection to the church and a support group to disciple them in their newfound faith.

Daughter Knows Best

Sandy attended one of our evangelistic meetings with her 7-year-old son. Hardly having ever attended church before, she had very little knowledge of the Bible and Christianity, but the Holy Spirit nudged her to come. She loved everything that she heard. At the end of the meeting we set the date of her baptism at her request. As a pastor I was in the habit of giving cards to those who get baptized to use to invite all their friends and relatives to the ceremony. I felt that baptism should be a time to cast the vision for evangelism. Those who come to witness the baptism became the new interests that the church worked with. Sandy sent out more than 50 invitations. One of the people who attended her baptism was her father.

Her father was secular with very little interest in Christianity, but he came to support his daughter. We often had a special celebration after every baptism. The father stayed for the special potluck and cake celebration. One of the godly men from our church sat beside him. They struck up a conversation with each other. Since they both loved fishing, they went out fishing the following Sunday. Three months later I had the privilege of baptizing Sandy's father! The *oikos* method proved its power again.

This story can be yours. You are the most effective evangelist for the people that you know: your neighbors, your sisters and brothers, your parents, your children, your coworkerrs, your friends. Because of that, you are their best opportunity to hear and receive the gospel. As a result, you can be the most effective evangelist in the world using the most effective type of evangelism in the world: the biblical method of *oikos* evangelism.

---

*Jurgen Goetzmann, "*Oikos*," *The New International Dictionary of New Testament Theology,* ed. Colin Brown (Grand Rapids: Zondervan, 1981), vol. 2, p. 250.

Chapter 11

Dying for Change:
The Challenges We Face Today

In the study we conducted regarding the devotional, ministry, and evangelistic practices of Seventh-day Adventists we discovered some disturbing trends that need to be addressed. As noted in the previous chapter, we found out that the most effective evangelists in the world are the people who are the closest to us. However, most of the time the followers of the Savior are not as intentional about sharing their faith as they should be. Many factors play out here, such as weak spirituality, lack of training, and, ultimately, lack of passion for God and people.

Challenges in the Church

What exactly are the challenges that we face in the church today? And how might we deal with them through God's strength?

1. Lack of consistent spiritual life. Our study (see table 1) reveals that only 73 percent of our active members pray on a daily basis and about 37 percent read the Bible on a consistent basis. When it comes to family worship, about 28 percent participate in it daily. Clearly the church has a great need to inspire, educate, and train our members in the area of spiritual growth. From my own observation, intentional discipleship is not happening, at least not in a consistent manner. As a pastor, I noticed that the members in my churches who were intentional about private devotional life as well as family devotional life tended to be happier, healthier, and more active in ministry and evangelism.

We hear much talk today about the need to train our members in the area of ministry and evangelism, and I agree wholeheartedly. However, if people are not passionate about God, the preparation they get will be mechanical and bland. But when they are fervent about God, nothing will stop them from doing ministry and evangelism. They will want guidance. What is important in the heart will become the center of life. When the heart is filled with divine things, it will spill over into life and action and will lead to sharing Jesus with others.

I believe that the leadership role in any church is to instill a vision for spirituality and to find creative ways to inspire the congregation to get passionate about spiritual growth. Leaders must also model a healthy spirituality, since personal example is indispensable in this area. As go the leaders, so go the people.

The heart of the Christian experience is to know Jesus Christ intimately. If we miss this, we've missed the point. Without an ongoing experience with Jesus, our faith falters, our growth ceases, and our witness to the world becomes ineffective. The research we have done tells us that as a church we're spiritually anemic and that most of us aren't bringing anyone to the Lord. It makes sense that those who pray and regularly read the Bible tend to be more effective in sharing their faith than those who don't.

Table 1
The Frequency of Participation in Devotional Practices

	Percentage
personal private prayer	
daily	73
once a week	21
personal Bible study	
daily	37
once a week	43
study of Sabbath school lesson	
daily	28
once a week	41
reading Ellen White books	
daily	14
once a week	29
never	57
family worship	
daily	28
once a week	33
never	39

2. Evangelism is not a core value for most of our members. Perhaps this is the area of our greatest challenge and need. Two thirds of our active members have not brought anyone to the Lord during a period of three years. The vast majority of our members are not engaged in any form of witnessing. As we look closely at the findings, we discover that only a small percentage of our active members actually volunteer to help with outreach events or programs or do something in the area of personal evangelism.

The role of leadership is to instill the joy of service, ministry, and evangelism in the hearts of our congregations. The power of vision is indispensable. In another research project we conducted we discovered that when leaders model and instill the vision for witnessing, the congregation will act accordingly and become more intentional about sharing their faith.

3. We are not doing well in attracting young people to the church. The data indicate an aging church. More than 60 percent of those who filled out the survey were more than 45 years of age, and 22 percent were 65 or older. Only about 9 percent were under 25 years old. I travel extensively in the United States, and most of the churches I visit are missing the 20- and 30-something age groups. Such data show the need for the denomination to be much more intentional about reaching and keeping young people in the church.

Table 2
People Our Members Brought to the Lord

How many people have you been wholly or partially responsible for bringing into the church in the past three years?

	Percentage
unaware of any	66
one	15
two to five	15
six to 10	2
more than 10	3

Reaching the Gen-X and millennium generations is not going to happen unless we make some serious changes in the way we do church. Leaders must not think of what they themselves like about church, but what they can do so that our young people feel comfortable and loved in it. The biggest change is in the area of spirituality. Young people are searching for a genuine, authentic community of faith. They are not looking for ritual or tradition, but for a power that transforms lives. First they want to see that Jesus has made a difference in our lives so that they can know for certainty that He will make a difference in their own.

4. We are not attracting or keeping new converts. The sample we studied consisted of longtime Adventists: 61 percent had been members for more than 20 years, and another 15 percent had been in the church from 11 to 20 years. Only about 4 percent had been members less than a year. Not only that, but 61 percent grew up with an Adventist parent. All this seems to indicate that our congregations are not attracting and bringing in many new members who have no Adventist background.

We must seek out new people. No matter what the church is doing, unless it is reaching people for the gospel, it has failed its mission. The church may have great buildings and wonderful music and fantastic schools, but if it does not bring people to God, it is not truly the church. When the church does its work well, it becomes the hope of the world and the source of grace. The church exists to bring people to the Savior and offer them the power of the Holy Spirit to change their lives. If we're not doing this, then what are we doing?

The Need for Change

We either continue doing what we're doing and become irrelevant, or with the courage of the Lord we change and plunge into a venture that will transform us and the world we live in. That will happen only when pastors, leaders, and members want it and cooperate to make it into a reality.

Move From Programs to People

Our research confirms that the most effective means of evangelism was and still is friendship and relationship evangelism. Moreover, the home still serves as a catalyst to make the gospel real to people. It is through relationships that we learn to apply the principles of the gospel to real life. Relationships, when they are healthy and intentional, will also help us see in a concrete way how to live the Christian life effectively and with joy. As people associate with us and see that we are better people because of Jesus—that we are better fathers or mothers, better husbands or wives, better sons or daughters—they are more likely to be attracted to Christianity than just by hearing doctrine or theology.

Thus the church must invest a great deal of effort in educating, training, equipping, and motivating our members to be passionate about sharing their faith with others. It should be a training ground to facilitate such endeavors. Observation and experience have convinced me that most churches pay very little attention to this.

What also often compounds the problem is that we give the impression that witnessing is going to strangers, knocking at their doors, and trying to convert them. Our members need to be inspired to share their faith naturally in whatever their context, whether it is the home, the marketplace, or the neighborhood. The most effective form of evangelism is the natural one, the one that takes place in the context of relationships. Andrew brought his brother Peter to Christ. We bring our loved ones to Him. When this happens, the new believers have the added advantage of having their own personal pastor-friend to minister to their spiritual needs.

Unfortunately, we have primarily focused on programs—smoking-cessation programs, Vacation Bible School programs, cooking school programs, food pantry programs, prophecy study programs. The list is long. Such programs are useful for inviting others to, but they lose much of their effectiveness when we don't know anybody to invite! It would be well for us to shift our emphasis to people and to building relationships with them. Then we would all be empowered to be the most effective evangelists, and our programs would have greater purpose and success.

Move From Just Doing Church to Spiritual Discipleship

To help our congregations capture a heart for God and cultivate the desire to know Him more intimately, we must employ everything possible, whether it be education, mentoring, or anything else. We cannot stop at getting people into membership: we need to move them into spiritual discipleship. Most of us take for granted that people will somehow grow spiritually without much instruction, guidance, structure, or mentoring. Or we may rely on the Sabbath sermon to do all the work of educating, motivating, and training to enable members to do all that they need to do to grow spiritually, but 30 impersonal minutes a week hardly seems sufficient. Our findings illustrate that in the area of spiritual practice we are weak and have a long way to go. Only 73 percent of our active members pray every day, a meager 37 percent have ongoing daily Bible study, and only 28 percent have daily family worship.

One of the churches I pastored started to decline about two years before I arrived. It experienced many conflicts involving direction and values. When I dug deep into the congregation's spiritual condition, I noticed more excitement at board meeting about trivial things than about Jesus and His mission. Discouraged about the state of the church and yet very hopeful about what God can do, I went to a board meeting with a vision to transform the church by focusing on spirituality. I wanted to do this by starting to have an extended time in the board itself for worship and prayer. For my first attempt, I prepared what I thought was a wonderful worship. But within just a few minutes one of the established members of the church stopped me and said, "As far as I am concerned, this is nothing but a waste of time. When are we going to get into the agenda?" In his understanding and that of many more, the agenda of the church had degenerated into making decisions about finances. That evening I went home extremely discouraged. After all, he had been an Adventist longer than I had been alive—maybe he knew something that I did not. But I also felt God telling me to keep at it. The church is all about connecting sinful people with God—of making Him real to them.

So I decided to continue the course. I started to preach about the need to connect with God on an intimate level. Right at the outset I discovered how difficult it is to turn the church into a holy place. Many in my congregation felt that I was trying to make the church too spiritual. Unfortunately, many others were just plain apathetic about spirituality.

But I determined to go forward no matter what. Not only did I live my faith—I became quite intentional about casting the vision for it continually. I preached about it and told stories about it. Over time the culture of the church shifted from maintaining the status quo to passion for God and for others. I faced many obstacles, and the members had to evaluate their priorities. Finally, though, we all grasped it. As the members became more spiritually healthy, more and more ministry and evangelism started to take place. The place shifted from apathy to purpose, from paralysis to prayer, from pain to promise. After about four years the church was totally transformed and started to grow. We went from a club with some spirituality to being the living body of Christ. It would not have been possible without a strong emphasis on spirituality.

Move From Programs to Purpose

Is it possible to be preoccupied with producing programs and yet miss their purpose? Perhaps your church is like many: very busy but with little to show for it, with members balancing maxed-out schedules yet seeing no results. The solution is probably not to add more programs that promise to be the key to unlocking your church's ministry potential. It is far better to maximize your congregation's strengths by focusing on a smaller number of ministries that you can do well and with purpose. This involves not just doing more or doing less or doing better—it is doing everything with the larger purpose of winning people to the Lord and building them up spiritually.

I felt that my role as a pastor was continually to instill the vision and educate and train members to be spiritual and intentional about sharing their faith. In the process I discovered that if I let this area slip by even for few weeks, the church suffered. Finally I came up with a plan to instill the vision at least once every week through preaching, testimony, sharing, songs, slogans, etc. Also I concluded that we needed a strategic approach to training. As a result we came up with a plan that every leader must train someone else to do the same ministry. I used to have monthly meetings with all the leaders of my church in their respective ministries for encouragement and training and to rejoice in what God had done in our midst.

Move From an Event Orientation to Process-focused Evangelism

One of the most prevalent misconceptions about evangelism is that it is an event: something that the church prepares for, does, and then recovers from! In the biblical paradigm, however, evangelism is not only what happens under a canvas tent. Evangelism is woven into the very fabric of the Christian's daily living, a process worked out in the lives of people over time.

Notice how the Bible teaches that evangelism is not the task of the few but a way of life for all. "Go and make disciples of all nations, baptizing them in the name of the Father and of the Son and of the Holy Spirit, and teaching them to obey everything I have commanded you" (Matt. 28:19, 20). "I pray that the sharing of your faith may promote the knowledge of all the good that is ours in Christ" (Philemon 6, RSV). The work of evangelism is the role and privilege of every believer. It is not the responsibility of the few who have gone to the seminary or have vast experience with soul winning.

Evangelism in the Book of Acts

An interesting exercise that I do in my training is to ask the question "When was the last time your church did evangelism?" The answer I get most often is "We had evangelistic meetings last year [or three years ago or 10 years ago]." As I mentioned earlier, most think of evangelism as an event rather than a way of life. In reality, evangelism takes place anytime, anywhere, any place, by anyone, under any circumstance.

Then I have them read the book of Acts and list all the times in which the believers did evangelism or ministry. Often they come up with more than 60 or 70 different incidents and methods of evangelism and ministry. The early church thought of evangelism not as an event but rather as the way they lived. They were excited about Jesus, and that is what made the difference. The early Christian church lived and breathed evangelism and ministry. Their ultimate core value was Jesus. The attitude of the early church was to win the world for Jesus and that nothing on earth would stop them. Their passion, occupation, and preoccupation were to turn the world upside down for Jesus Christ. Thus their evangelism was the outflow of their daily living.

Move From Stagnation to Innovation

Though research has shown that the most effective method of evangelism is through relationships, we still need multiple ways to influence people for Jesus. Our own studies indicated that many of the following programs scored high in their effectiveness: public evangelism (36 percent), books (49 percent), television or radio (20 percent), Bible correspondence courses (19 percent), and Internet (7 percent). (See "How People Join the Church," p. 115.)

Having a variety of evangelistic methods serves at least three purposes. The first is to create many avenues for the believer to share his or her faith in a natural way. The second is to reach multiple groups of people when any one method might not appeal to all of them. The third is to venture out of our *oikos* (see chapter 10) and find new and receptive seekers who are outside of our current circle of relationships.

In the research we conducted to identify the fastest growing Adventist churches and what has made them effective, we discovered that all growing churches employ multiple evangelistic avenues. They use Sabbath school, the worship service, multiple miniseries, seasonal events (Christmas, Easter, Mother's Day, Father's Day, etc.), sporting events, and personal and public evangelism to reach seekers. The study shows that healthy and effective churches combine at least nine pathways[1] and entryways[2] a year to reach the community. The church must use every means it has to reach people. Every event, every ministry, every activity, should have as its purpose connecting others with God.

Personal and public evangelism should complement each other, neither being used without the other. If the church is intentional about growth, it also must employ multiple pathways and entryways to reach people. It is not only the events used for evangelism that count—it is how they are conducted. A Sabbath school class could be for discussion or be repurposed for evangelism. When the leaders decide that the Sabbath school is for evangelism, they will be intentional about inviting seekers, use lessons that appeal to them, and employ an atmosphere and language conducive for evangelism. From this perspective, everything that a church does can be made evangelistic.

Move From Paralysis to Prayer

The research we conducted to identify the fastest growing SDA churches revealed that many pastors and congregations struggle with discouragement. Many have not experienced any baptisms for a year or more. Some are not growing, and many are actually declining. If you are in that situation, do not give up. Try prayer and watch what God can do.

One day I received a card in the mail from a woman requesting Bible study. I took Fred, one of our members, with me for training. When I knocked on the door, a vivacious individual in her early 40s opened it. Showing her the card, I asked her if she wanted to study the Bible. "I did not send this card," she replied.

"Well, would you like to study the Bible anyway?" I continued.

"No, I am not into these things." So I asked if she would allow us to pray for her, and she consented.

After we prayed for her, we got into the car and started to drive away. As we were leaving the driveway, she ran after us, yelling, "Stop, stop! I am not interested in studying the Bible, but my neighbor across the street is. I will take you there now." When we went across the street, a woman, 73 years old, drunk and smoking, greeted us. I asked her if she would like to study the Bible. Well, she did not have anything to do, so she said yes. Fred and I started to study the Bible with Ann. I did it reluctantly because of my allergies to tobacco smoke and because of her age, since older people have a more difficult time receiving Christ. But to my surprise, she accepted Him as her Lord and Savior.

Later on she gave up her smoking and drinking. A few weeks later she got baptized. Fred and I visited her the day after her baptism to cast the vision for ministry, evangelism, and soul winning. "Ann, do you have a family?" I asked.

"I have a huge family."

"God has a mandate for you. He wants you to win your family to Him."

"How I am going to do that?"

"Pray about it, and God will show you."

About three and a half years later our union conference sent their communication director to shoot a video of Ann on Sabbath morning, surrounded with the people that she had led to the Lord. Picture the scene with me: Ann stood in the middle of the platform surrounded by 57 people, including Jena, the woman who had refused to study the Bible with Fred and me.

The union communication director went around asking the 57 people, "Why are you an Adventist today?" He got one answer, "We saw the change in Ann's life, and we wanted it." Then he turned to Ann. "What did you do to win your family and friends to the Lord?"

"I prayed for them day and night. Then the Lord showed me many ways to strengthen my relationship with them and meet their needs. When the time was right, I invited them to church, or to a Bible study or an evangelistic meeting. Every time one of them became a Christian, that person joined me in praying for the rest. God has been so good to us."

This is the power of prayer—the power of an ongoing process. It is the power of *oikos* and of personal spirituality. Yes, we face many formidable barriers in church growth today, but God's grace is might—and available to you!

---

[1] Pathways are events that take place during a long period of time and have strong spiritual emphases, such as Sabbath school classes for seekers or evangelistic meetings.

[2] Entryways are events that take place in a short time, such as cooking seminars or stop-smoking classes.

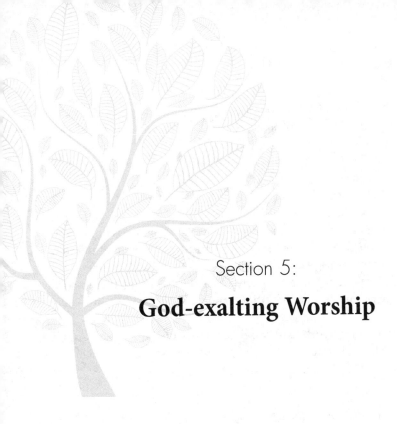

Section 5:

God-exalting Worship

Bring About Worship Renewal

Church renewal is always connected with worship renewal.[1] While it has always been true, it is much more so today. James Emery White in *Opening the Front Door: Worship and Church Growth* observes that church growth and renewal are always connected with the worship experiences.[2] We learned from our interviewing that most people are hungry for powerful, vibrant, energetic worship. Many long to have an encounter with God, to feel His presence and live His power. Every time the church is intentional about prayer, building discipleship, and bringing about worship renewal, it becomes healthy and starts growing.

George Barna[3] makes it clear that the number one expectation that people have of the church is to feel God's presence. Knowing this, let us shift our attention from programs to spirituality, discipleship, and relationship building. We urge our congregations to pay much more attention to their worship services and bathe them with prayer and the presence of true worshippers who themselves experience the presence of God. Thom Rainer found that inspiring worship services contribute in a highly positive way toward evangelism, discipleship, and new member assimilation.[4]

The following chapter covers the finding of our interviews with about 230 people across the spectrum to learn what makes a worship service a God-exalting one. Seven major factors emerged. The people:

(1) experienced the presence of God
(2) experienced the grace of God
(3) were inspired with hope
(4) felt loved by the community of faith
(5) were transformed
(6) were challenged to service
(7) enjoyed excellence

At the end of each section I give some practical suggestions on how to improve your worship service and make it inspiring and energetic and thus turn your sanctuary into a place where people exalt God and feel His grace and presence. These lists come from my observation and interviews with pastors, members, and leaders of various churches, as well as with some seekers.

If you are a leader, work hard to bring about worship renewal. And if you are a member, experience the presence of God so that you will become a contagious Christian.

---

1 Walter Kaiser, Jr., *Quest for Renewal: Personal Revival in the Old Testament* (Chicago: Moody Press, 1986), pp. 11-25.

[2] James Emery White, *Opening the Front Door: Worship and Church Growth* (Nashville: Convention, 1992), pp. 62-64.

[3] George Barna, lecture, Adventist Ministerial Convention, Myrtle Beach, S.C., January 2009.

[4] T. S. Rainer, *High Expectation Churches,* p. 20.

Chapter 12

The Worship Experience
Your Heart Longs For

It's Sabbath morning, 11:00. For the next hour or so you'll be sitting in church, in another worship service. What do you expect from it?

An opening song, followed by the invocation, leading into the welcome and announcements. Prayer, offering, Scripture reading, some singing, and a sermon.

Yes, but what do you *want* from worship?

That's what we desired to know. As we studied the subject of worship and of growing Adventist churches, we interviewed 230 people,[1] asking them three specific questions:

1. What makes a worship service a good one?
2. What do people expect from the worship service?
3. What kind of experience should people leave with as they exit afterward?

Today no church growth can take place apart from dynamic and inspiring worship,[2] a fact that became clear to us in our study of thriving Seventh-day Adventist congregations. We discovered that all of the expanding Adventist churches emphasized the worship experience and invested time, creativity, and variety into it. No one style of worship stood out above all the rest[3]—rather it was the quality of the worship experience that mattered.

What Is Worship?

Before we deal with the factors that make a worship experience a God-exalting one, we need to know more about worship itself, particularly corporate worship. Worship is an active response to God whereby we declare His worth. It is not passive, but participative. Nor is it just a mood or feeling. Instead it is a response in obedience and commitment to Him, a declaration about His works and goodness. Therefore our worship experience should lead us to a better relationship with Him as we respond in love, adoration, praise, and obedience.

The English word "worship" is expressive of the act that it describes. It comes from the Anglo-Saxon *weorthscipe*, which then was modified to "worthship," and finally to "worship." Worship means "to attribute worth" to something or someone. When we say of someone that "he worships his money" or that "she worships her children," we are employing the word a bit loosely. If, however, the supreme worth for him is in his money, or the highest value for her is in her children, then it is an accurate use of the word. To worship someone or something is to attribute supreme worth or to declare supreme value to that individual or thing. Should we elevate this thought to the realm of divine-human relationships, we have a working definition of worship ready-made for us. To worship God is to ascribe to Him supreme worth, for He alone is worthy. We want to live in such a way that we exalt and glorify God in all things. Worship is a way of life rather than primarily ceremony.[4]

Corporate worship occurs when the healthy church gathers regularly as the local expression of the body of Christ to worship God in ways that engage the heart, mind, soul, and strength of the people. All creation exists to bring glory to God, but only humanity has the ability to do it out of a loving relationship with God as our Father. It means that we have been uniquely created for His love. Our bringing glory to God flows out of our love for Him. The Old Testament associated worship with the house of God. Yet in the New Testament Christ Himself makes the profound statement that God is seeking out those who will worship Him in Spirit and truth, who seek to accomplish His original purpose.

Every worship experience, whether personal and corporate, should inspire us to experience God in a fresh and meaningful way. It should lead us to the throne of grace, at which we receive hope and new life and will be inspired to do ministry and service.

The Essential Qualities of a God-exalting Worship Service

Now that we have defined worship, let us look at what makes it God-honoring and -glorifying. Below are seven important qualities of a God-exalting worship service that surfaced in our interviews with both members and religious seekers. Pastors, leaders, and members need to experience authentic worship and do whatever it takes so that everyone else will share it. A pastor or church leader bears heavy responsibilities to make sure that the worship service is truly a God-exalting and -honoring experience. If you are a member, please get close to God so that you might sense His presence and power, because others want to see Him in you.

1. Experience the presence of God. Again and again people told us that they want to enjoy God, that what they desire most from worship is to truly sense His presence. Many people are looking for an experience with God—to live in His power and be touched by His grace and love[5]— and they'll go anywhere to find it. Why don't we make our churches the place people can encounter the Lord and begin enjoying Him forever?

God's desire is to be with His people. It's how He spent His time in the Garden of Eden (Gen. 3:8), it's why He called for a wilderness tabernacle (Ex. 25:8), it's one of the many reasons that Jesus came to earth (John 1:14), and it will be the glory of the new earth (Rev. 21:3; 22:1–5).

Yet the privilege of God's presence was not limited to Adam or ancient Israelites or first-century Galileans, nor is it a gift that we receive only upon entrance to the New Jerusalem. Jesus has promised that when people gather in His name, He is there among them (Matt. 18:20). Every worship service, every meeting conducted in His name, holds the promise of His presence, so when your church assembles together, God is there too.

It would be well for us to focus more on creating a holy climate through prayer, music, and education that will help people become aware of the divine presence. Many worshippers come to church looking for more than fellowship, exhortation, or exposition. Such individuals arrive seeking an experience with the Holy One. They look for "awe and reverence, mystery and transcendence." What is your church doing to provide that opportunity?

We experience God's presence through prayer and by being in contact with other people who also perceive Him. Those thriving churches that help their congregations feel the presence of God do it through prayer, praise, music, an atmosphere of loving acceptance, good greetings and welcome, and by using worship leaders who have a personal relationship with Him. Today growing churches seek to find a balance between content and emotion, working to create a worship service that ministers to both the head and the heart, one in which worshippers can learn about God and yet also meet with Him—sing about God and also sing to Him.

To move your worship service toward better facilitating an experience with God,[6]

- **develop an atmosphere of praise,** not of conflict.
- **emphasize adoration** and thanksgiving in your worship service. Don't just give information.
- **aim for the mind and the heart,** not one to the exclusion of the other.
- **communicate from personal experience** how to experience God.

2. Experience the Grace of God. "In six days the Lord made the heavens and the earth, the sea, and all that is in them" (Ex. 20:11), but the Lord God is more than just an impersonal force of the universe. Notice the *way* that He created. For six days He used His voice to speak creation into existence, sending out His divine, omnipotent utterance. The voice is meant to be heard—words are spoken in order to be understood. Even as He was forming the world by the power of His word, God was communicating, expressing His personhood.

And though He generated all else by the sound of His speech, on the sixth day the Lord used His hands to shape man out of the dust of the ground and employed His own breath to give him "the breath of life" (Gen. 2:7). Talk about a personal touch! And what could be more personal than an entire day set aside for communion with Him? God's gift of the Sabbath to the human race is a powerful weekly reminder that our God is personal, relational, and interested in us.

The people we interviewed told us that when they go to church they want to connect with such a personal God—to know that He cares for them deeply and intimately, that Jesus really loves them. They long to know His grace, to know that it is sufficient for them and that salvation can be theirs.

How do we experience grace in worship? How do we come to know the truth of the gospel in our own lives? We need to hear it (again and again and again), and we must receive the message through people who have also experienced it. Here are some practical steps you can take in your worship service to offer the water of the gospel to your grace-parched community:

- **Invest in the spiritual development of your worship leaders.** If they don't know grace, they can't share it.
- **Include a gospel presentation in every sermon and teaching.** In a creative and compelling way, tell and retell the story of Jesus. We too easily forget the truth that God loves us and that we matter to Him, so remind your hearers again and again of the basics of God's love and His salvation by grace.
- **Celebrate God's living grace through personal testimonies.** This takes the promise that "His grace is sufficient for me" out of the theoretical and into the vivid personal.
- **Thank God for His loving grace during corporate prayer.** While balanced worship includes confession and lament over sin, we can put people in touch with the reality of God's grace by thanking Him for it.

3. Be inspired with hope. In a world filled with 24-hour news stations and crises at the personal, national, and global levels, the church must be a place of refuge. As His body, the community of His people, we can be a place of new beginnings and second chances.

Lyle Schaller, a Christian researcher and church consultant, says that if you offer a promise of hope, your church attendance will grow by 20 percent.[7] A woman confessed, "My husband beats on me emotionally all week, and I want to go to church to receive a note of hope." As people slip into the pews on Sabbath morning, they've come hoping that they've entered a sanctuary, a place to receive divine comfort and encouragement.

Are you sharing a gospel of hope? It is hard to be enthusiastic about a church that criticizes everything about you. But it is much easier to inspire people to live for Jesus if we offer them the good news of grace, hope, love, and forgiveness. People will come to Jesus and be willing to change in the safety of a loving place.

How can your worship service instill hope in the participants? Here are some practical ideas:

- **Find your own personal hope in Jesus Christ.** As a church member (whether Pastor Pierce or Paul Pewsitter) you are the most influential element in the atmosphere of your congregation. Get grounded in Christian hope, and God will use you to offer His encouragement to others.
- **Infuse hope in every sermon and in Sabbath school teaching, as well as during prayer meeting and Bible study.** No topic in the world is so discouraging that Jesus doesn't have the solution for it. Whether you're preaching from Lamentations or rebuking personal sin, make sure you lift up Jesus as our only hope.
- **Make room for joy.** "These things I have spoken to you, that My joy may remain in you, and that your joy may be full" (John 15:11, NKJV). Whether through prayer or music or greeting or visual aids, put the Christian's joy into your service.
- **Practice forgiveness.** Unless your congregation has an attitude of forgiveness, the message of hope in your church's worship service will be choked out by bitterness and anxiety—no matter how many praise choruses you may sing.

4. Feel loved by the community of faith. "This is My commandment, that you love one another as I have loved you" (verse 12, NKJV). Even for a commandment-keeping people, those are some tough words to hear! Still, of all places, the church must be where people are loved.

If you ask them, as we did, people will tell you that they want a friendly church, but the research shows that the definition of friendly has changed. In the past, being friendly meant being nice: saying hello, acting courteously, handing out bulletins. Today it means offering acceptance and respect for the person. It stands for community in a safe and loving environment, the totality of the experience of going to church. Whether people attend church in a blue suit or blue jeans, whether they show up with a bottle of water or a cup of cappuccino, whether they quote Ellen G. White or Oprah, they will find themselves welcomed, respected, and valued.

I have been to a lot of churches, some of them full of warmth, love, and a spirit of acceptance; some of them harsh and full of backbiting; and some of them perfectly happy just with each other, with no desire to bring in any guests. But I have never heard any of them say, "We're critical and faultfinding and not as loving as we should be" or "We're friendly with each other, but we tend to alienate visitors and thus we're not as loving as we should be." Every church says they're a loving church. Based on the definition below, can your congregation honestly be called loving?

A loving church is . . .

- defined by the quality of caring, not the formality of the greeting time.
- a "home" where one's fears, joys, yearnings, and aspirations can be shared without risk of condemnation and rejection.
- a supportive community for those who are struggling.
- A place for friends who can be trusted, depended upon, and enjoyed, and who share the same goals.
- a place where God's love is experienced in a concrete way through His people.
- a place where imperfections do not lead to rejection and people discover their greatest potential.
- a place where people are open and honest together without the fear of being judged.
- a place where distinctions of personal rights, possessions, thoughts, emotions, and actions are secondary to a commitment to each other and to the kingdom of God.
- a place where people laugh with others, not at others; cry with others, not because of others; forgive others, and are forgiven by others; love others, and are loved by others.

Through God's grace and power your church can become a caring and warm community of faith in which all kinds of people are accepted and loved, a place where members are excited about being there and bringing their friends with them. The result is that when people attend our churches, they will have a feeling of belonging and intimacy.

5. Be transformed. The activity of most churches centers on the Sabbath morning service, popularly called the "worship hour." But that does not guarantee that people are really worshipping! Worship is responding from the heart to God for whom He is and what He has done.

Each time we encounter God afresh He changes us. True worship results in life transformation. It brings us closer to God, reveals our sinful nature and our need for Him, and motivates us to ask Him to change us. Worship never allows us to remain the same person, because it impacts us in several ways:

- **heart response.** No worship is legitimate unless it comes from the heart. In worship we give God the worth that He is due. The Lord could see through the hypocrisy of His people in Ezekiel's time, denouncing their empty praise: "With their mouth they show much love, but their hearts pursue their own gain" (Eze. 33:31, NKJV). God is more impressed with our hearts than our mouths.

- **transformed life**. God expects worship to translate into life change. With sadness in His voice He tells His messenger Ezekiel, "Indeed you are to them as a very lovely song of one who has a pleasant voice and can play well on an instrument; for they hear your words, but they do not do them" (verse 32, NKJV). When we genuinely worship in His presence, we repent of sin and deepen our relationship with Him.

- **raising the bar.** Genuine worship regularly calls for a greater sacrifice from the worshipper. When worshippers feel God's presence and hear His voice, they follow His call to go deeper in Christ than they have previously experienced.

We can give people the opportunity to respond during song service, by coming forward during the congregational prayer, in the giving of tithes and offerings, through the final hymn, or in a closing appeal in the sermon. Every part of the worship service can be crafted with the goal of transformation in mind.

6. Be challenged to service. In the Greek language of the New Testament the word for service can also be a word for worship. Worship and service go hand in hand. At its best worship always motivates the worshipper to live a holy life filled with ministry to others.

The prophet Isaiah was in the Temple worshipping God when he heard the angels singing, "Holy! Holy! Holy!" It moved him to confess his sins, a confession followed by the assurance of his pardon. Then the voice of God declared, "Whom shall I send? And who will go for us?" Deeply touched, Isaiah replied, "Here I am! Send me!" (see Isa. 6).

True worship will always result in service. Christians often make the mistake of limiting their worship to one hour each week, but God is no less worthy the rest of the time! One way to worship Him all week is through a life of service and ministry to others. Every worship gathering must include a challenge to service. People need to apply what they have learned and experienced during the worship hour.

7. Enjoy excellence. One Friday night I received a call from a member of the church where I had recently become the pastor. "What's your sermon for tomorrow about?" she asked.

"I'm preaching on the book of Hosea."

"And what is going to be the theme of your sermon?"

"I will be preaching on the love of God."

Thanking me, she then hung up.

Intrigued, I called her back and asked about her interest in my sermon. She told me that her Lutheran family was coming to visit for the weekend. While she considered inviting them to church, she "wanted to make sure the sermon wouldn't be off the wall." The woman sought to make certain that what I said wouldn't embarrass her or turn off her visiting family.

And that's really not too much to ask, is it?

Today, when people demand excellence, churches often settle for mediocrity. "It's just church" seems to be the sentiment, as if what happens there is not that important or as if uninspired worship is good enough. Yet to give our least in our worship of the Most High is definitely not good enough.

How does God feel about the worship offering that your team and your congregation bring every week? Is it done in the Spirit and in truth? Or is it done in Friday night dashes and Sabbath morning improvisation? A simple diagnostic question is this: Are you excited to invite people to your church? (For tools to help your leadership team assess and develop worship in your church, see Appendix B, "Worship: Reflection and Assessment.")

Here are some ideas that will help improve the excellence of your worship services:

- Recruit worship teams of people who are fully engaged with God.
- Begin a talent development process.
- Plan at least a month in advance, even up to a year beforehand.
- Have one theme running through the whole service.
- Rehearse your services.
- Communicate using images, props, and audio elements.
- Invest the time needed to prepare inspiring sermons.[8]
- Eliminate dead time.
- Freshen the look of the service: bright decor, bright lighting, and adequate sound.

Christians have many reasons for worship. We worship because of what God has done, is doing, and will do through His Son, Jesus Christ, and through His Spirit. According to Revelation 14:6-12 worship is the commemoration of creation and a celebration of the gospel. It is the believer's response to divine mercy and goodness through the act of adoration, reverence, thanksgiving, obedience, and submission.

God's greatness and the beauty of His grace are powerful, life-changing, and worthy of celebration. That's what our hearts desire to experience when we come together for a religiouis service, and it's what God longs to give us in His name.

---

[1] The group of interviewees included about 15 pastors, 40 leaders, and 40 members from growing churches and equal numbers from plateauing or declining congregations, and about 40 seekers from the same geographical area. As mentioned previously, we defined a growing church as a congregation that is experiencing a 3 to 5 percent increase in membership, baptisms, and attendance for a minimum of three years.

[2] T. S. Rainer, *Effective Evangelistic Churches,* pp. 115, 116.

[3] See also Robert Webber, *The New Worship Awakening: What's Old Is New Again* (Peabody, Mass.: Hendrickson, 2007), p. 13.

[4] S. Joseph Kidder, *Majesty: Experiencing Authentic Worship* (Hagerstown, Md.: Review and Herald, 2009), pp. 19, 20.

[5] A reality confirmed by other researchers, e.g., Glen Martin and Gary McIntosh, *The Issachar Factor: Understanding Trends That Confront Your Church and Designing a Strategy for Success* (Nashville: Broadman and Holman, 1993), p. 39.

[6] This list and all the rest in this chapter are the composite of what healthy and growing churches do to provide a dynamic and inspiring God-exalting worship services to their members and seekers.

[7] Lyle E. Schaller, *44 Ways to Increase Church Attendance* (Nashville: Abingdon, 1988), pp. 23-25.

[8] Thom S. Rainer notes that while the average pastor may spend as little as two hours per week in sermon preparation, pastors of growing churches invested around 22 hours a week developing their messages (*Surprising Insights From the Unchurched,* pp. 67, 220-222).

Section 6:

Where to Go From Here?

Two questions beg to be answered. The first one is "What did we learn from our research?" We discovered that church growth is God's will and is possible through His power. First and foremost, it is God's movement on His people, His church, and His world. Second, the most effective evangelists in the world are you and me. God has called us to work side by side with Him. The influence of a committed believer is beyond measure. No one can be where you are, and no one can influence your family and friends as well as you can. Third, church growth happens best when believers are proud of their church and passionate about their Lord. Fourth, four major components must work together to make the church an exciting place to be. They are: leadership that believes in the God of the impossible and is willing to train and cast the vision for evangelism; the power of prayer that moves on the hearts and leads people to Jesus; active laity that share joyfully their faith; and a church in which God is exalted, honored, and worshipped with awe and reverence.

The second question is what to do with this information. I have put together 10 easy steps that I pray will revive your church and make it what God intended it to be. Anything you do is better than nothing.

Chapter 13

The First 10 Steps

In the previous pages we have looked at the ingredients that make a church a healthy, growing, and attractive place to belong to. The questions that many people raise at this point are Where do we go from here? What can my church do to move forward? How can we be transformed into an exciting place where God is glorified, the members are on fire for Him, and religious seekers find a place to call home? Here are my suggested steps.

Ten Steps

1. Pray a lot. A fantastic future for your church begins with prayer. To labor without serious prayer, no matter how intelligent or diligent our efforts, will result in more of the same: human-size attainments and a nagging sense that there's got to be something more to church than this. If we take the word of the Lord seriously, then we will heed His message in Zechariah 4:6: "'Not by might nor by power, but by My Spirit,' says the Lord of hosts." Prayer is a nonnegotiable first step to church renewal and growth.

We want our churches to be God-directed, so let's begin by asking Him where He wants to go. In addition to our regular devotional practices, we must devote an hour every day to praying for our church, for its leaders, for the community, for wonderful blessings from God. Pray for wisdom and a vision from the Lord about His dreams for our congregations. Ask God to show us how He wants to glorify Himself through our church. Our task as spiritual leaders is not merely to guide and direct people, but to guide and direct people into God's way.

2. Cultivate spirituality. We must prioritize healthy, growing spirituality above attendance numbers or any other measurement of success. In our endeavors to revive our churches or reverse the declining numbers, Christians attempt all kinds of solutions: introducing programs, changing clergy, writing new policies, designing different strategies, adapting what worked in other places. Gilbert R. Rendel, researcher and senior consultant with the Alban Institute, argues that none of this works. Meaningful, lasting change is spiritual change.[1]

An emphasis on spirituality and revival should be the main work of the church, and this calls for much greater investment in the spiritual development of our pastors, leaders, and members. The most important earthly asset that the church has is its people. When they are spiritually healthy, growing, trained, and equipped, they will do great things for God. As vividly described in the book of Acts, fully devoted followers of Jesus Christ will joyfully give everything to God and His purpose.

Part of cultivating spirituality is to approach all of the church's work—from Vacation Bible School to Sabbath school teachers' meetings to work bees—as essentially kingdom work. If it is not kingdom work, then stop doing it! But if it is, then communicate that sense of excitement and sacredness as you do your own tasks. At the same time, affirm others for their kingdom work too. Above all, keep reminding yourself and others that the ministry of the church is not only important but eternal.

3. Embrace faith-based optimism. God can do amazing and awesome things. He created the universe and continues to uphold it by the power of His word (Heb. 1:3), so doing wonderful deeds is exactly what He specializes in. Faith in the living God and in His powerful Word absolutely makes a difference in the health and direction of a church. So embrace the hopeful expectation that your Christian faith provides, and pass it along to every other member of your faith community. Convey this faith-based optimism in all of your official and unofficial communications. Tell and retell the facts of the situation: "God can do the impossible—and He wants to do it here!"

4. Cast the vision of the dream church. God has a dream for your church, and it's at least everything that you've wished it could be. Imagine a place where people are experiencing the gospel, a community filled with prayer and the power of the Holy Spirit, an agent of eternal change in your local community, a church in which worship is exciting and everyone is willing to share with those in need. In your personal prayers, ask God for a vision of what your congregation could be through Him. It will be an exciting concept!

Then share that vision with your fellow believers. Awaken in their hearts a desire for this dream church. Describe something that makes them say: "I want to give my life for that cause! I would give my time, my money, and my talents for that church! I would love to be a part of that." Arouse them to a sort of holy dissatisfaction with the way things presently are. Many people have had only fleeting hopes of a dream church and instead have accepted the status quo, thinking, *It's just the way things are.* But with the Lord Jesus Christ it doesn't have to stay that way. Cast the vision of the dream church, and people will resonate with it—and this will bring energy to your congregation.

5. Build up relationships with existing leaders. Strife or distance between leaders will trap a church into plateau or decline. The relationship between leaders goes a long way in determining the effectiveness of the organization they lead. For a church that means beginning with the biblical injunction to love one another as Christian brothers and sisters and then strengthening those ties.

Make sure you're on the same team headed for the same goal. Build strong relationships with positional leaders (those people with official titles) and influential leaders (those who may not have a title but still have significant sway in the congregation).

6. Be a leader maker. Nothing will happen without leaders. They are those inspiring individuals who do ministry, give strength to the church system, organize the efforts of the group, cast the vision, and mentor and train the members. Without leaders for children's ministries, for example, there will be no one to vision or dream, no one to plan the curriculum, no one to teach, no one in charge of the crafts or snacks, no one to ensure that goals are being met. In short, there would be no children's ministry and no young families moving to your church.

And if building up leaders seems too time-intensive or too troublesome, remember that Jesus invested the bulk of His earthly ministry in the lives of a small group of His disciples, and it was those disciples that led the church in the power of the Spirit after His death. Time, effort, and resources spent in the recruitment, training, and empowering of leaders in your congregation will give abundant returns.

7. Start improving things. You may be surprised at the big effect that even small improvements can have on the atmosphere of your church. It may be repainting the primary classroom or redesigning the bulletin or weeding the front flower beds, but all such seemingly small upgrades send a big message: this is a place worth investing in. They also act as small "wins" for the congregation, a necessary element for a church that will be experiencing a lot of change in the next few years. Members need to see that things are already starting to get better and that they can begin feeling a healthy sense of pride in their church.

8. Improve your worship service. As noted previously, church renewal is always connected with worship renewal. While it has always been true, it is even much more so today.[2] After many interviews with individuals, it became clear to us that most people are hungry for dynamic and inspiring worship. Many are longing to have an encounter with God, to feel His presence and live His power. As long as this hunger remains primary, the worship service will be the fundamental criterion on which they evaluate the church. For this reason alone it deserves special, prayerful attention.

Though people are eager to feel the presence of God, many in our churches do not experience it. As we examined successful congregations, it became apparent that every time churches are intentional about prayer, building discipleship, and bringing about worship renewal, they become healthy and start to grow. Widespread research supports this fact, demonstrating that the worship service contributes in a highly positive way toward evangelism, discipleship, and new member assimilation.[3] As an example, one Adventist church increased its attendance by more than 700 people when it focused on worship renewal and added another worship service aimed at meeting the needs of the people.

9. Simplify the church process. The fundamental objective of church structure and policies ought to be fulfilling the gospel commission, bringing the good news of Jesus Christ into the lives of the people in the world. Many reported to us that they experienced the church structure as more of a barrier to ministry than a help. Remove as many possible layers of bureaucracy for those that have ideas for new ministries or want to get involved in existing programs. Make it as easy as possible to witness, to serve, to get training, to find resources, to start something new.

10. Utilize critical thinking. Taking regular time to reflect on one's personal ministry and on the progress of the congregation toward God's vision is a much-neglected task of spiritual leadership, but it is necessary to be continually evaluating what is being done and then looking for ways to do it better. I recommend taking two hours every week to reflect on your own ministry. *How well have you done this week? Did you meet your goals for yourself? Did you fulfill God's calling for you? How can you preach better? What can you do to better communicate the gospel to those inside and outside of your church? Are your meetings effective? Are they Christ-centered and spiritual?* Evaluate the past week and look to improve, by God's abundant grace, the next one.

In addition to your personal reflection time, it is useful to discuss the strengths and weaknesses of the church and its activities within a group setting.[4] When you meet with the board, ask for their evaluation of you and of what the church has been doing. Be open to their criticisms and recommendations. Since they're thinking it anyway, you might as well benefit from it. The same principle works well in other groups, too: the Sabbath school council, the elders, the youth group, and even the social committee. Never assume that anything you've done is perfect, and be willing to give praise to the Lord when people are blessed in spite of the imperfection!

Furthermore, effective leaders practice critical thinking and do not merely reflect other people's ideas, plans, programs, or vision. Too often pastors, swamped by a busy schedule and eager to see something change, do too little critical thinking and too much wholesale borrowing. In their effort to grow the church they copy existing models and focus their energies on promoting programs. Then, sadly, programs—not saving souls—become the mission of that church.

Assessing their particular situation, asking critical and thoughtful questions, and coming up with solutions to meet the urgent needs of our time is the heart of leadership. A spiritual leader always faces three basic questions: Where is God in action so that we can join in with Him? How can we be more effective in what we do? What are we doing that is not effective anymore? (And then we need to have the courage to terminate what is no longer adequate, or repurpose it so that it will be.)

Conclusion

Our research shows major disturbing trends in Adventism in the North American Division in the area of church growth. The denomination is experiencing a decline in the rate of expansion as compared to membership and to the rate of increase in the population. It is also taking more and more financial resources to produce a single convert.

The challenges that the church faces today are varied and serious, yet as we consider the way to move forward in the future it is crucial for us to understand that our greatest need can be supplied by only one source: the Lord Jesus Christ. Through the ages the church has always had some serious challenges both from inside and outside—from persecution, compromise, dissention, secularism, apathy, and worldliness. Yet God has promised that He will be with us constantly and even until the end of the age (Matt. 28:18-20). He has assured us that the church will go on to triumph because it is "the one object upon which God bestows in a special sense His supreme regard."[5] With His blessing, your dream church can become a reality.

The greatest need of the church today is not a new program, but a new passion; not to live in the past, but to engage in the present and visioning for the future; to rely not on human effort, but on divine power. The missional calling of the church today will be fulfilled not by the use of worldly methods and ideas, but only through a connection with the Lord Jesus Christ, who said that without Him we can do nothing, but with Him we can do all things (John 15:1-5). So as we journey into the future, let us go with Him. The best days of the church are still ahead of us.

---

[1] Gilbert R. Rendel, *Leading Change in the Congregation* (Alban Institute, 1998), pp. 35-37.

[2] W. Kaiser, Jr., *Quest for Renewal,* pp. 11-25.

[3] T. S. Rainer, *High Expectation Churches,* pp. 174, 175; G. Barna, lecture, Adventist Ministerial Convention, January 2009.

[4] For a helpful, biblical discussion guide, see Appendix C, "God's Exam for Churches and Church Leaders."

[5] Ellen G. White, *The Acts of the Apostles* (Mountain View, Calif.: Pacific Press, 1911), p. 12.

The Search for Promising Leaders

Spotting a New Leader

Here are 12 ways to identify future leaders. I call them 12 signs of potential.

1. Leadership in the past. The best predictor of the future is the past.

2. The capacity to create or catch a vision. A person who doesn't feel the thrill of a challenge is not a potential leader.

3. A constructive spirit of discontent. Have you ever thought about what that better way might be?

4. Practical ideas. Leaders seem to be able to identify which ideas are practical and which aren't.

5. A willingness to take responsibility. Leadership is about the joy of accomplishment—the vicarious feeling of contributing to other people.

6. A completion factor. When the work comes in, it gets finished. A half-cooked meal isn't good enough.

7. Mental toughness. No one can lead without being criticized or without facing discouragement.

8. Peer respect.

9. Family respect.

10. A quality that makes people listen to them.

11. A solid commitment to the Lord and the church.

12. A strong spiritual walk with God. A good leader will have a Christlike character and wisdom, and be filled with grace.

Four Character Checkpoints

1. Does this person want more to be liked or to honor God?

2. Does this person have a destructive weakness or sin?

3. Can this person accept reasonable mistakes without being discouraged or giving up?

4. Can I provide this person the environment to succeed?

Worship: Reflection and Assessment

Beginning Questions

Improving a worship service ultimately comes down to practical changes, but it doesn't start there. With something as sacred as the worship of our God as His church, we would do well to start thinking through the purpose of worship. Here is a set of questions for a worship team or leaders to work through as they begin their work of evaluating and developing their worship service.

- What is the purpose of our worship?
- What is the significance of worship in the life of a Christian disciple?
- What do we "expect" that worshippers in our church will experience when they worship here?
- What do we actually want people to experience when they worship here?
- What is the focus of our worship?
- Whom is our worship about? Whom is it for?
- What is the role of God, Jesus, and the Holy Spirit in our worship experiences?
- How well do we "teach" worship? How well do we model it?
- How do we help people recover a communal sense of worship as the role of the people of God rather than as a collection of individuals?

Post-Service Worship Evaluation

To keep the worship service grounded in its purpose and to maintain excellence, here are questions that your worship team can use for a five- to 10-minute evaluation afterward.

1. How well did we fulfill our purpose in worship today?

2. What can we do to improve the quality of our worship service? Bring out the strengths.

3. What did we do that did not improve the quality of our worship service? Eliminate the weaknesses.

4. Is our worship understood by the first-time visitor and urgent enough for both the believer and the seeker?

5. Where is the God-moment of our worship and what can we do to make sure that it happens with the highest intensity and the most clarity? This is the time in our worship service that we have a vision of God—it is the moment our hearts touch His.

God's Exam
for Churches and Church Leaders
(Based on Ephesians 4:11-16)

These biblical questions are useful at board meetings and training events.

1. What of eternal significance happens in the lives of individuals while they are in the care of your church? (verse 11)

2. In what ways are your members ministering? (verse 12)

3. What percentage of your members are involved in ministry? (verse 12)

4. Do your members' ministries result in the spiritual growth of faith, knowledge, and maturity? (verse 13)

5. Do the lifestyles of your members reflect the principles and character of Christ? (verse 13)

6. What percentage of your members' lifestyles reflect that of a growing Christian? (verse 13)

7. What percentage of your members are easily shaken in their faith and vulnerable to deceitful schemes? (verse 14)

8. Does your church experience spiritual and numerical growth? (verse 15)

9. Do your members mutually edify and build up one another? (verse 16)

10. What can you do to be faithful to the instruction of Scripture?